DIGIBYTE

HISTORY OF THE FIRST YEAR

A DECENTRALISED PAYMENT NETWORK
PART OF THE "ALT-ERNATIVE" BOOK SERIES

DigiByte—History of the First Year

by Christopher P. Thompson

Book Author by Christopher P. Thompson

Book Design by C. Ellis

ISBN—13: 978-1519602800
ISBN—10: 1519602804

DIGIBYTE

HISTORY OF THE FIRST YEAR

A DECENTRALISED PAYMENT NETWORK
PART OF THE "ALT-ERNATIVE" BOOK SERIES

CHRISTOPHER P. THOMPSON

ABOUT THE AUTHOR

Christopher Paul Thompson is an avid cryptocurrency enthusiast from the United Kingdom. Born in Bradford, UK and academically educated at the University of York (BSc Mathematics). He has been a keen follower of past and current events in the crypto space since March 2013. His first book called Cryptocurrency "The Alt-ernative" A Beginner's Reference is the first book he has ever written.

Other titles currently available:

"Peercoin—History of the First Year"

"Reddcoin—History of the First Year"

Other titles planned for release are:

"Dogecoin—History of the First Year"

"Quark—History of the First Year"

"Dash—History of the First Year"

"Cryptographic Decentralised
Currencies and Assets—
The "Alt-ernative" Book"

E-mail Contact: chris_thompson25@live.co.uk

Twitter Contact: https://twitter.com/MrSilverCider

CONTENTS

CONTENTS

INTRODUCTION

Cryptocurrency was born with the advent of Bitcoin. It was first mentioned in a research paper published online titled "Bitcoin: A Peer-to-Peer Electronic Cash System" with the real name or pseudonym Satoshi Nakamoto attributed to it. This paper was published on the 31st of October 2008. About two months later on the 3rd of January 2009, the Bitcoin network protocol was launched. This technological breakthrough was the beginning of a decentralized public ledger. It allows people to send value across the globe without the permission of a third party authority.

Since then, a growing number of people around the world have been introduced to or discovered cryptocurrency. Many cryptocurrencies have been launched over the following years since the introduction of Bitcoin. The name "alternative" was given to these cryptocurrencies after Bitcoin because they were developed, implemented and introduced to be used instead of or alongside Bitcoin. One could say, a choice of brand in cryptocurrency exists. People have discovered these either through word of mouth, by accident, through personal investigation or via the media. Nevertheless, it has changed the lives of many people. It has provoked the general public into asking innumerable questions about many issues based on subjects such as economics, politics, philosophy, mathematics and so on.

In this book, I hope to give the reader insight into how one particular alternative cryptocurrency began. DigiByte began in early 2014 as a Scrypt proof of work clone of Litecoin. This book, as well as other future books to be written on other cryptocurrencies, is a historical story of the first year. It covers the time from the initial announcement on Bitcointalk up until the blockchain had been publicly available for one year. In this case, from the 10th of January 2014 to the 12th of January 2015. It also describes the terminology one encounters in cryptocurrency such as proof of work mining, block reward, wallets and so on.

INTRODUCTION

I chose to write about just the first year for various reasons, some of which are:

- For almost all cryptocurrencies, the first year of their existence is the most defining period.

- If I had chosen to write a full history of DigiByte, I would be continuously playing catch up.

- Most other cryptocurrencies are not several years old yet, so I have limited the scope of all books on individual cryptocurrencies at this time.

- Currently I have a full-time job besides being a cryptocurrency author, so my time is unfortunately limited.

You may have bought this book because DigiByte is your favourite cryptocurrency. Alternatively, you may be keen to find out how it all began. I have presented the information henceforth without going into too much technical discussion about DigiByte. If you would like to investigate further, I recommend that you read material currently available online at the official website at www.digibyte.co.

If you choose to purchase a certain amount of DigiByte, please do not buy more than you can afford to lose.

Enjoy the book :D

WHAT IS DIGIBYTE?

DigiByte is a cryptocurrency or digital decentralised currency used via the Internet. It is described as a payment network without the need for a central authority such as a bank or other central clearing house. It allows the end user to store or transfer value anywhere in the world with the use of a personal computer, laptop or smartphone. Cryptography has been implemented and coded into the network allowing the user to send currency through a decentralised (no centre point of failure), open source (anyone can review the code), peer-to-peer network. Cryptography also controls the creation of newly mined DigiByte units of account.

The DigiByte network protocol was created by using the source code inherent in the original Scrypt based coin called Litecoin. The developers of DigiByte altered the code to produce an alternative coin with a differing block reward schedule, block time, difficulty re-targeting algorithm and total number of expected coins.

On the official DigiByte Bitcointalk thread, DigiByte is described as:

"DigiByte 极特币 (DGB) is a rapidly growing worldwide decentralized payment network & digital currency, inspired by Bitcoin. DigiByte allows you to move money over the internet similar to PayPal & Western Union but with many improvements, including lightning fast transactions with minimal or no fees. You send & receive DigiBytes to or from any DigiByte address in the world in a matter of seconds with no required sign up, registration, or hidden fees."

The slogan used by the DigiByte community to market the coin is:

"YOU STORE & SEND DATA IN MEGABYTES & GIGABYTES, WHY NOT SEND MONEY IN DIGIBYTES"

IS DIGIBYTE MONEY?

Money is a form of acceptable, convenient and valued medium of payment for goods and services within an economy. It allows two parties to exchange goods or services without the need to barter. This eradicates the potential situation where one party of the two may not want what the other has to offer. The main properties of money are:

♦ **As a medium of exchange**—money can be used as a means to buy/sell goods/services without the need to barter.

♦ **A unit of account**—a common measure of value wherever one is in the world.

♦ **Portable**—easily transferred from one party to another. The medium used can be easily carried.

♦ **Durable**—all units of the currency can be lost, but not destroyed.

♦ **Divisible**—each unit can be subdivided into smaller fractions of that unit.

♦ **Fungible**— each unit of account is the same as every other unit within the medium (1 DGB = 1 DGB)

♦ **As a store of value**—it sustains its purchasing power (what it can buy) over long periods of time.

DigiByte easily satisfies the first six characteristics. Taking into account the last characteristic, the value of DigiByte, like all currencies, comes from people willing to accept it as a medium of exchange for payment of goods or services. As it gets adopted by more individuals or merchants, its intrinsic value will increase accordingly.

WHY USE DIGIBYTE?

Like all cryptocurrencies, people have chosen to adopt DigiByte as a medium of exchange through personal choice. An innovative feature of the coin, an affinity towards the brand or high confidence of the community could be reasons why they have done so. Key benefits of using DigiByte are:

- It is a useful medium of exchange via which value can be transferred internationally for a fraction of the cost of other conventional methods.

- DigiByte eliminates the need for a trusted third party such as a bank, clearing house or other centralised authority (e.g. PayPal). All transactions are solely from one person to another (peer-to-peer).

- DigiByte has the potential to engage people worldwide who are without a bank account (unbanked).

- DigiByte is immune from the effects of hyperinflation, unlike the current fiat monetary systems around the world.

Fourteen reasons why the developers/community think DigiByte is the cryptocurrency of choice are:

"Security: DigiByte uses five highly advanced cryptographic algorithms."

"Speed: DigiByte transaction notifications occur in 1-3 seconds, blocks are discovered every thirty seconds and transactions are fully confirmed every 3 minutes. Future planned upgrades will make these times even faster."

"Fees: Most DigiByte to DigiByte transactions are free or carry a very small network-mining fee to incentivize people to mine."

"Worldwide: DigiBytes are already stored, traded and transacted in over 89 countries."

WHY USE DIGIBYTE?

"**Decentralization:** There is no need for a third party or central server."

"**Re-Spend:** Send DGB you received to someone else in as little as three minutes."

"**Finite Production:** New DigiBytes are added to the network every thirty seconds through a process called mining as each new block (or grouping of transactions in a spreadsheet like format) is discovered by the network."

"**Scarcity:** 21 Billion DigiBytes will be created in 21 years."

"**1% Monthly New Minting Reduction:** New DigiByte production decreases 1% every month."

"**Mining:** DigiByte mining is decentralized with five independent, highly secure mining algorithms."

"**Adaptable, innovative & flexible:** DigiByte is constantly adding new features & services to remain on the cutting edge of digital currency technology."

"**Committed Development:** DigiByte has been under constant, progressive development for over one year now with core development team members from all over the world."

"**Millennial Acquisition Potential:** DigiByte provides merchants, banks & other legacy institutions with a new means of acquiring & connecting with tech savvy millennial users."

"**A Bright Future:** DigiByte has many new & exciting projects underway to be released throughout 2015 to increase DigiByte utility and new user adoption across the globe."

DIGIBYTE SPECIFICATION

Since the birth of DigiByte, its coin specification has changed a few times. At the time of publication of this book, its current specification is:

Coin Symbol:	DGB
Unit of account:	DGB
Date of Announcement:	10th of January 2014 07:42:30 UTC
Genesis Block Generated:	10th of January 2014 21:13:14 UTC
Block Number One Generated:	10th of January 2014 22:27:56 UTC
Date of Launch:	12th of January 2014 17:24:55 UTC
Founder:	Jared Tate
Lead Developer:	"DigiByte"
Hashing Algorithms:	SHA256, Scrypt, Skein, Groestl & Qubit
Timestamping Algorithm:	Proof of Work
Address Begins With:	D
Total Coins:	21 billion DGB in 21 years
Block Time:	15 seconds
Difficulty Retarget Time:	60 seconds (DigiShield)
Coins per Block:	(see pages 24 and 25)
Confirmations per Transaction:	6
Pre-mine:	0.5% (105 million DGB)

DIGIBYTE MILESTONE TIMELINE

10th of January 2014	—DigiByte announced on Bitcointalk forum.
10th of January 2014	—DigiByte Facebook group created.
10th of January 2014	—DigiByte blockchain began at 22:27:56 UTC.
12th of January 2014	—Public launch of the blockchain at 17:24:55 UTC.
12th of January 2014	—DigiByte Subreddit created.
13th of January 2014	—Original Twitter page created @DigiByte2.
16th of January 2014	—Jared Tate interviewed by Brendon Lindsey.
17th of January 2014	—Cryptokopen began to trade DGB.
19th of January 2014	—Coin Market began to trade DGB.
21st of January 2014	—Android wallet released on the official website.
24th of January 2014	—Android wallet released on Google Play Store.
29th of January 2014	—Cryptorush.in began to trade DGB.
1st of February 2014	—User "bman3" released DigiMan mascot designs.
2nd of February 2014	—First known DGB transaction for goods/services.
5th of February 2014	—CryptX.io began to trade DGB.
6th of February 2014	—Coined Up began to trade DGB.
6th of February 2014	—DigiByte added to www.coinmarketcap.com.
12th of February 2014	—MintPal began to trade DGB.
18th of February 2014	—OpenEx began to trade DGB.
23rd of February 2014	—DigiByte v2.0 (DigiShield) client released (mandatory).
28th of February 2014	—Block schedule altered at block number 67,200.
2nd of March 2014	—Comkort began to trade DGB.
4th of March 2014	—AllCrypt began to trade DGB.
12th of March 2014	—DigiShield successfully implemented into Dogecoin.
14th of March 2014	—Paper wallet site www.digiaddress.com went live.
14th of March 2014	—Swisscex began to trade DGB.

DIGIBYTE MILESTONE TIMELINE

14th of March 2014	—Cryptsy began to trade DGB.
15th of March 2014	—AGX.io began to trade DGB.
15th of March 2014	—Prelude by Moolah began to trade DGB.
20th of March 2014	—Cryptokk began to trade DGB.
22nd of March 2014	—Prelude by Moolah introduced direct USD trading.
23rd of March 2014	—Over 30 million DGB transactions surpassed.
28th of March 2014	—Windows v2.9 wallet client released (not mandatory).
7th of April 2014	—EuropEx began to trade DGB.
9th of April 2014	—Jared Tate spoke at the Cryptocurrency Convention in New York City.
15th of April 2014	—CryptoCzar began to trade DGB.
18th of April 2014	—A total of one billion DGB surpassed at 11:21:29 UTC.
30th of April 2014	—DigiByte v2.9.1 wallet client released.
2nd of May 2014	—DigiByte mentioned live on CNBC "Fast Money"
8th of May 2014	—DigiByte TipBot on Reddit went live (/u/dgbTipBot).
9th of May 2014	—DigiByte mentioned live on CNBC for the second time.
31st of May 2014	—Algorithm change decision made.
16th of June 2014	—Mining algorithms Groestl, SHA-256, Scrypt and Qubit chosen as definite parts of the upcoming Multi-Algo.
20th of June 2014	—An algorithm switch successfully tested at a specific block (mined on all five algorithms on testnet)
24th of June 2014	—DigiByte Team attended the "Inside Bitcoins" conference in Hong Kong.
7th of July 2014	—The only block reward reduction in July.

DIGIBYTE MILESTONE TIMELINE

29th of July 2014	—DigiByte Team attended the first ever "Digital Currencies Convention for Bankers" in New York City.
14th of August 2014	—DigiByte version 3.0.0 (Multi-Algo) released.
16th of August 2014	—DigiByte version 3.0.1 (Multi-Algo) released.
20th of August 2014	—Bittrex began to trade DGB.
1st of September 2014	—Block number 145,000 successfully reached.
3rd of September 2014	—LiteBit.eu began to trade DGB.
29th of September 2014	—CEX.IO began to trade DGB.
11th of October 2014	—A total of 2 billion DGB surpassed as being mined.
14th of October 2014	—Cryptsy initiated the DGB/XRP trading pair.
20th of October 2014	—DigiByte version 3.0.2.1 wallet client released.
18th of November 2014	—Jared Tate interview by Deemington published.
27th of November 2014	—DigiByte version 3.0.3 wallet client released.
28th of November 2014	—New offices opened in Santa Monica, California and Hong Kong.
28th of November 2014	—A private investment of $250,000 made to DigiByte.
4th of December 2014	—A total of 3 billion DGB surpassed as being mined.
10th of December 2014	—Hardfork at block number 400,000 occurred.
10th of December 2014	—Cryptopia began to trade DGB.

YEAR 2015

10th of January 2015	—One year since the blockchain began.
12th of January 2015	—One year since the blockchain was launched publicly.

DIGIBYTE BLOCKCHAIN

Every cryptocurrency has a corresponding blockchain within its decentralised network protocol. DigiByte is no different in this sense. A blockchain is simply described as a general public ledger of all transactions and blocks ever executed since the very first block. In addition, it continuously updates in real time each time a new block is successfully mined. Blocks enter the blockchain in such a manner that each block contains the hash of the previous one. It is therefore utterly resistant to modification along the chain since each block is related to the prior one. Consequently, the problem of doubling-spending is solved.

As a means for the general public to view the blockchain, web developers have created block explorers. The first block explorer for DigiByte was made available at the website http://altexplorer.net on the 13th of January 2014. A few others were created afterwards, but no longer exist.

Since the inception of the first block explorer, other websites have been created. Currently available block explorers include the following:

- http://digiexplorer.info/;

- https://prohashing.com/explorer/Digibyte/;

By visiting and browsing these two explorer sites, only the first one is specifically for DigiByte. It is the official block explorer of DigiByte. One can easily access the site by visiting the official DigiByte website at www.digibyte.co and then scrolling to the bottom of the homepage. At the bottom left, there is a direct link under "Block Explorers" which reads "DigiExplorer (Insight)"

DIGIBYTE BLOCKCHAIN

Block explorers tend to present different layouts, statistics and charts. Some are more extensive in terms of the information given. Some statistics include:

- **Height of block** —the block number of the network.

- **Time of block** —the time at which the block was timestamped to the blockchain.

- **Transactions** —the number of transactions in that particular block.

- **Total Sent** —the total amount of cryptocurrency sent in that particular block.

- **Block Reward** —how many coins were generated in the block (added to the overall coin circulation).

Below is a screenshot of block number one from the block explorer at http://digiexplorer.info/:

Number Of **Transactions**	1
Height	1 (Mainchain)
Block Reward	72000 DGB
Timestamp	Jan 10, 2014 10:27:56 PM
Merkle Root	dd8a4a3b8ecdc14e4142ffb73a5b0c...
Previous Block	0

PROOF OF WORK (PoW) MINING

Proof of work mining is a competitive computerised process which helps to maintain and secure the blockchain in such a way as to verify transactions and prevent double spending.

In the general sense of cryptocurrency, those who participate in the activity of mining are called miners. They are general members of the cryptocurrency community who dedicate processing power (hash) of their computers towards solving highly complex mathematical problems and verifying transactions. This process upholds the integrity and security of the network. As such, miners are described as protectors of the network. Each transaction (held within a certain block) is validated before adding it to the blockchain. By doing this, they are rewarded (as an incentive) with newly generated mined coins or transaction fees. These coins are issued by the software in a transparent and predictable way outside of the control of its founders and developers. A miner can be based anywhere in the world as long as they have an internet connection, sufficient knowledge of how one mines and the hardware/software required to do so.

Miners use GPUs (Graphical Processing Units) or CPUs (Central Processing Units) to process transactions by hashing. Also, Application Specific Integrated Circuits (ASICs) allow miners to use customised hardware for faster and lower power mining.

Originally, the DigiByte hashing algorithm was solely Scrypt until the 1st of September 2014. As a consequence of the release of v3.0 of the wallet client, a hard fork changed the hashing algorithm at block number 145,000. Instead of one single algorithm, miners were then able to mine DigiByte via five independent algorithms. At the time of publication, these algorithms, which constitute the Multi-Algo hashing algorithm, are Scrypt, SHA-256, Groestl, Qubit and Skein

BLOCK TIME OF DIGIBYTE

The block time is the average time taken for the network to successfully generate a certain block either by proof of work or proof of stake. Both the reward and time of all blocks generated dictate how the circulation of coins grows over time.

Originally, the block time of the network protocol was pre-determined to permit miners to find one block every 60 seconds (on average). This remained the case after the first hard fork (DigiShield) took place on the 28th of February 2014. The first twelve blocks timestamped to the blockchain on the 10th of January were:

Block Number 1	22:27:56 UTC		Block Number 7	22:36:27 UTC
Block Number 2	22:32:35 UTC		Block Number 8	22:38:34 UTC
Block Number 3	22:32:41 UTC		Block Number 9	22:39:40 UTC
Block Number 4	22:33:16 UTC		Block Number 10	22:41:48 UTC
Block Number 5	22:35:09 UTC		Block Number 11	22:46:40 UTC
Block Number 6	22:35:31 UTC		Block Number 12	22:46:56 UTC

As is evident above, it took nineteen minutes to find the first twelve blocks.

On the 1st of September 2014, the block time changed from 60 to 30 seconds. Obviously, this had the effect of speeding up the number of blocks timestamped to the blockchain. The developers thought this was necessary. They wanted to make sure that the number of DGB mined was as close to 4 billion (target) as possible before the end of 2014.

On the 10th of December 2014, the third hard fork did not alter the block time. Instead, the reward per block reduced by about 64% to 2,434.41 DGB at block number 400,000. Also, the reward has continued to reduce by 1% every 80,160 blocks (approximately every month) since that time.

BLOCK REWARD DISTRIBUTION TABLE

Below and on the adjacent page, the block reward distribution table for the first year is shown. There were 38 block reward reductions during this time including two reductions due to hard forks. DigiShield initiated a reduction of 0.5% at block number 67,200 and the third hard fork called MultiShield caused a ~64% reduction at block number 400,000.

During the first year, a total of about 3,342,203,514 DGB were mined.

First Block	Last Block	Number of Blocks	Date of Initial Block	Time of Initial Block UTC	Block Reward	Generated Coins	Cumulative Total of Coins
0	0	1	10/01/2014	21:13:14	0.000000	0	0
1	1,439	1,439	10/01/2014	22:27:56	72000.000000	103,608,000	103,608,000
1,440	1,526	87	12/01/2014	01:05:11	16000.000000	1,392,000	105,000,000
1,527	5,759	4,233	12/01/2014	17:24:55	16000.000000	67,728,000	172,728,000
5,760	67,199	61,440	15/01/2014	00:45:37	8000.000000	491,520,000	664,248,000
67,200	77,279	10,080	28/02/2014	22:52:17	7960.000000	80,236,800	744,484,800
77,280	87,359	10,080	10/03/2014	14:40:18	7920.200000	79,835,616	824,320,416
87,360	97,439	10,080	22/03/2014	08:37:21	7880.599000	79,436,438	903,756,854
97,440	107,519	10,080	02/04/2014	23:13:38	7841.196005	79,039,256	982,796,110
107,520	117,599	10,080	15/04/2014	12:22:29	7801.990025	78,644,059	1,061,440,169
117,600	127,679	10,080	29/04/2014	20:56:29	7762.980075	78,250,839	1,139,691,008
127,680	137,759	10,080	20/05/2014	23:39:26	7724.165174	77,859,585	1,217,550,593
137,760	147,839	10,080	07/07/2014	04:54:35	7685.544349	77,470,287	1,295,020,880
147,840	157,919	10,080	02/09/2014	19:55:26	7647.116627	77,082,936	1,372,103,816
157,920	167,999	10,080	07/09/2014	00:46:50	7608.881044	76,697,521	1,448,801,337
168,000	178,079	10,080	11/09/2014	18:00:14	7570.836639	76,314,033	1,525,115,370
178,080	188,159	10,080	16/09/2014	12:02:04	7532.982455	75,932,463	1,601,047,833

BLOCK REWARD DISTRIBUTION TABLE

First Block	Last Block	Number of Blocks	Date of Initial Block	Time of Initial Block UTC	Block Reward	Generated Coins	Cumulative Total of Coins
188,160	198,239	10,080	20/09/2014	16:14:20	7495.317543	75,552,801	1,676,600,634
198,240	208,319	10,080	24/09/2014	16:03:51	7457.840955	75,175,037	1,751,775,671
208,320	218,399	10,080	28/09/2014	16:59:18	7420.551751	74,799,162	1,826,574,833
218,400	228,479	10,080	02/10/2014	14:28:52	7383.448992	74,425,166	1,900,999,998
228,480	238,559	10,080	06/10/2014	11:27:50	7346.531747	74,053,040	1,975,053,038
238,560	248,639	10,080	10/10/2014	08:40:52	7309.799088	73,682,775	2,048,735,813
248,640	258,719	10,080	14/10/2014	06:38:01	7273.250093	73,314,361	2,122,050,174
258,720	268,799	10,080	18/10/2014	01:37:35	7236.883842	72,947,789	2,194,997,963
268,800	278,879	10,080	21/10/2014	21:43:14	7200.699423	72,583,050	2,267,581,013
278,880	288,959	10,080	25/10/2014	21:47:58	7164.695926	72,220,135	2,339,801,148
288,960	299,039	10,080	29/10/2014	17:12:05	7128.872446	71,859,034	2,411,660,183
299,040	309,119	10,080	02/11/2014	03:18:48	7093.228084	71,499,739	2,483,159,922
309,120	319,199	10,080	05/11/2014	17:01:31	7057.761944	71,142,240	2,554,302,162
319,200	329,279	10,080	09/11/2014	11:41:00	7022.473134	70,786,529	2,625,088,691
329,280	339,359	10,080	13/11/2014	06:22:36	6987.360768	70,432,597	2,695,521,288
339,360	349,439	10,080	17/11/2014	01:02:13	6952.423964	70,080,434	2,765,601,721
349,440	359,519	10,080	20/11/2014	22:29:58	6917.661845	69,730,031	2,835,331,753
359,520	369,599	10,080	25/11/2014	00:18:13	6883.073535	69,381,381	2,904,713,134
369,600	379,679	10,080	28/11/2014	21:00:25	6848.658168	69,034,474	2,973,747,608
379,680	389,759	10,080	02/12/2014	18:28:53	6814.414877	68,689,302	3,042,436,910
389,760	399,839	10,080	06/12/2014	17:58:49	6780.342802	68,345,855	3,110,782,766
399,840	399,999	160	10/12/2014	15:33:24	6746.441088	1,079,431	3,111,862,196
400,000	480,159	80,160	10/12/2014	16:51:45	2434.410000	195,142,306	3,307,004,502
480,160	560,319	80,160	07/01/2015	15:22:32	2410.065900	193,190,883	3,500,195,384

FIRST YEAR DIGIBYTE EXCHANGES

Throughout the first year, twenty known cryptocurrency exchanges added DigiByte to their trading platform. These were:

Cryptokopen.eu	EUR	CLOSED	17th of January 2014
Coin Market	BTC	CLOSED	19th of January 2014
Cryptorush.in	BTC	CLOSED	29th of January 2014
CryptX.io		CLOSED	5th of February 2014
Coined Up	BTC	CLOSED	6th of February 2014
MintPal	BTC	CLOSED	12th of February 2014
OpenEx		CLOSED	18th of February 2014
Comkort		CLOSED	2nd of March 2014
AllCrypt		CLOSED	4th of March 2014
Cryptsy	BTC and XRP	ACTIVE	14th of March 2014
Swisscex		CLOSED	14th of March 2014
AGX.io		CLOSED	15th of March 2014
Prelude		CLOSED	15th of March 2014
Cryptokk		CLOSED	20th of March 2014
EuropEx	BTC	CLOSED	7th of April 2014
CryptoCzar		CLOSED	15th of April 2014
Bittrex	BTC	ACTIVE	20th of August 2014
LiteBit.eu	EUR, USD and GBP	ACTIVE	3rd of September 2014
CEX.IO	BTC	ACTIVE	29th of September 2014
Cryptopia	BTC and LTC	ACTIVE	10th of December 2014

CURRENT DIGIBYTE EXCHANGES

A cryptocurrency exchange is a site on which registered users can buy or sell DigiByte against BTC, LTC, USD and so on. Some exchanges require users to fully register by submitting certain documentation including proof of identity and address. On the other hand, most exchanges only require users to register with a simple username and password with the use of a currently held e-mail account.

On the 23rd of November 2015, there were seven known exchanges or methods to buy/sell/trade DigiByte. At this time, Cryptsy was the exchange on which trading of the coin has lasted the longest (since the 14th of March 2014).

Since the 10th of January 2014, a total of fifteen known exchanges have closed down due to server problems, hackings or other dubious activities.

Poloniex and ShapeShift incorporated DigiByte in the second year. At the time of publication of this book, the coin enjoys the vast majority of its daily trading volume on Poloniex. Besides Cryptsy and Bittrex, these three constitute almost 100% of all DigiByte trades with either BTC, LTC or another cryptocurrency.

Current cryptocurrency exchanges which actively allow users to trade DGB are:

Exchange	Location
Cryptsy	United States
Poloniex	United States
Bittrex	United States
CEX.IO	United Kingdom
LiteBit.eu	The Netherlands
ShapeShift	Switzerland
Cryptopia	New Zealand

DIGIBYTE WALLETS

A wallet is basically a piece of software that can be used on a personal computer, tablet or smartphone. It allows users to store DigiBytes as well as execute transfers of DGB with other users. Alternatively, it can be described as a means to access the coins from the inseparable blockchain (public transaction ledger). The wallet cryptographically generates and holds the public and private keys necessary to make these transactions possible. The software can be accessed, downloaded and installed from the official website by selecting "Choose Wallet" at the top of the homepage at:

* http://www.digibyte.co/

DigiByte wallets have been developed to work on the operating systems Windows, Mac OS X and Linux. Currently, there are four types of wallet available to the community. These are:

* **Mobile & Web Wallets:** The easiest way to send and receive DigiBytes and to make payments is through a DigiByte mobile wallet.

* **Desktop Wallets:** The true power of the DigiByte network resides in users running a desktop client. If you want to help DigiByte grow stronger, more secure and more decentralised run a desktop wallet.

* **Gaming Wallets:** The DigiByte Gaming wallet is an easy to use, marketing friendly way to bring new users into DigiByte from outside of the existing digital currency community.

* **Linux Wallets:** Pretty much all of the services and core infrastructure for the DigiByte network runs on a linux wallet. If you are a developer, you know digibyted.

VIEW OF JARED TATE

Founder/Creator of DigiByte

How did DigiByte originally begin? "After discovering Bitcoin in the fall of 2012 I spent the majority of my spare time over the next year learning all I could about Bitcoin and its source code. By November of 2013 I decided it would be a good idea to start a project that would help improve the bitcoin protocol and make it better.

In your opinion, what makes DigiByte stand out from other cryptocurrencies? "DigiByte as it stands today is faster, more available, more scalable, more decentralised and poised for more growth in 2016/2017 than any other cryptocurrency I know."

How have you helped the promote DigiByte? "I feel being honest and transparent since day one, as well as publicly known has done more to keep the DigiByte project alive through the ups and downs than any other one specific thing. We have a solid track record to stand on that anyone can publicly verify."

What was your most memorable about of DigiByte from January 2014 to January 2015? "Launch day without a doubt. I remember I scheduled the launch for 12 PM (MST) on a Sunday after pre announcing the launch several days before. At that point I had no idea what would happen when the network went live and the wallets were released and mining started. In hindsight things went really well compared to most of the launches I have witnessed of other cryptocurrencies. I would attribute that to detailed planning & testing ahead of time. It was by far the most stressful day I can remember to date. It is probably the closest I will ever be to actually giving birth."

Where do you see DigiByte in the near to distant future? "By the end of 2016 I see DigiByte making a lot of headway with millennial customers in the gaming, remittence and e-commerce markets. I also see DigiByte joining a handful of "top" cryptocurrencies as the market continues to further consolidate moving forward. By 2035 I see DigiByte handling 100,000 TPS worldwide."

VIEW OF 24HRALTTRADE

Michael (24hralttrade), DigiByte Community Liason , Netherlands

"I am the founder and owner of a clothing store, The House of Blue Jeans - Tofugear Omnitech Demostore

I started trading digital currency at the beginning of 2014 and first discovered DigiByte in June 2014. I started mining DGB at the beginning, and currently hold a long-term investment in DigiByte. It is the only digital currency investment that I own at the moment.

From the beginning I noticed the professional approach of Digibyte and the continuous hard work of founder Jared Tate. Jared has always been open to the community and is always looking for better ways to get Digibyte into the mainstream adoption.

After they announced the investment I knew Digibyte is on the right path and the future is looking bright. Around March 2015 Jared and Tofugear came to The Netherlands to talk about Digibyte and the Tofugear Omnitech Platform.

After this meeting I received the message that Tofugear wants to start the omnitech platform at House of Blue Jeans and after a couple of months the Tofugear team came to my store for 14 days to install the whole platform. Long days and hard work but the result is amazing!

I'm sure Digibyte is on the right track. The community grows every day and the developments keep coming. Digibyte Gaming will breach the doors for mainstream adoption of Digibyte and together with Tofugear they will build the future of micropayments.

Digibyte - Breaking Barriers, Building Bridges"

VIEW OF ROB FEHN ("RJF")

"I discovered DigiByte in March of 2013 while looking for a coin that showed professionalism, commitment and long term appreciation. First post on the forum in June. DigiByte has always had a professional "feel" to it. The principles are capable, civil and 100% committed to the project, the main reasons I started buying, trading, and mining, DBG. There are only a few others in the market with this type commitment to quality and service. You don't need "high tech" to succeed, just high standards.

I think one of the things that really stands out from the early days is Jared. His constant presence in the forums and regular videos sold me on DBG early on. If he said it was so, or it would be so, there was no doubt it would happen. The future? I see DBG in a rather elite group of ALTs that will not only survive but, prosper in the various use categories that are developing. I won't go so far to predict price but, I will predict success!"

VIEW OF EPLDCC

"Starting 2014 I was filled with optimism about digital currencies. They seemed to hold the promise of a better future. I was filled with hope. I had been mining for about a year and I cashed out some of my savings to place a couple of preorders for ASIC mining equipment. After I placed the orders I was so excited I spent the next few weeks planning how I would spend what I believed would be unending mining rewards.

Within a few months, all my hopes faded away. Mt. Gox collapsed, and with it the values of bitcoin and altcoins. While the difficulty levels continued to rise the corporate mines and multi-pools took advantage of the small home miners. The original delivery dates for my orders passed; and, by the middle of the summer, I figured I had lost all my money. Instead of hope, I felt betrayed and disgusted at the greed and corruption.

In September of 2014 I received one of the ASIC systems. Then I saw the news of the DigiByte fork to multi-algorithm mining. All of a sudden, I could mine DigiByte. I was impressed with the DigiByte forum. Here, was a digital currency doing everything right. DigiByte reminded me why I had been hopeful about digital currencies. DigiByte reminded me of the professionalism and community values that had drawn me to digital currencies. I converted all my digital currency to DigiByte, I switched all my mining to DigiByte; I told a couple of my friends and they were also happy to get involved. DigiByte is the best decision I've made in all my experiences with digital currencies. Since then, I've watched the progress and innovations, I started the DigiByte Group to support the community, and we all continue to realize the opportunities created by DigiByte."

VIEW OF IIKUN

How did you discover DigiByte? "One day I was browsing the altcoins sub-forum on Bitcointalk and came across the DigiByte thread. Right away DigiByte struck me as a different product altogether to the many cut and paste coins being floated every day. The developer Jared (although we didn't know his name back then) was very involved and wasn't simply looking for a quick profit. DigiByte was the first cryptocurrency I mined solo and I found my first block on January 17, 2014."

In your opinion, what makes DigiByte stand out from other cryptocurrencies? "The key is Jared's determination to keep differentiating from other cryptocurrencies, and it's possibly the principle reason I've stayed involved. Also the community - whenever problems arise they get discussed (relatively) calmly, and solutions are developed and implemented."

How have you helped the promote DigiByte? "I was involved in the Bitcointalk thread from the end of week one. I pushed several app developers for DigiByte's inclusion on their iOS based coin-ticker apps and although I had to step asidefor a while due to work I've always remained active in some capacity. I'm also a moderator at DigiByteForum."

What was your most memorable about of DigiByte from January 2014 to January 2015? "Aside from mining my first DigiByte block, for me it was the release of DigiShield. It really proved the developer was in with us for the long-haul."

Where do you see DigiByte in the near to distant future? "I see DigiByte's real growth coming in the medium term, perhaps as early as late 2016, as people learn about its superior functionality and question Bitcoin's suitability for commercial transactions; DigiByte's near-instantaneous confirmations will be a key driver of its success. Similar to Bitcoin in its early days, DigiByte has proven it has one of the strongest, vibrant and most positive communities in crypto."

DIGIBYTE COMMUNITY

A community is a social unit or network that shares common values and goals. It derives from the Old French word "comuntee". This, in turn, originates from "communitas" in Latin (communis; things held in common). DigiByte has a community consisting of an innumerable number of individuals who have the coin's well being and future goal at heart. These individuals almost always prefer fictitious names with optional corresponding "avatars". Notable members of the community are Jared Tate, "24hralttrade", "HR", "Jumbley" and "EPLDCC".

At the time of publication, there are social media sites on which discussion and development of DigiByte take place. These are:

- **Facebook**   -www.facebook.com/DigiByteCoin

- **Official Forum** -http://www.digibyteforum.com/

- **Reddit**   -https://www.reddit.com/r/Digibyte/

- **Twitter**   -www.twitter.com/DigiByteCoin

- **YouTube**   -www.youtube.com/DigiByteCoin

In addition to these, there is the official forum thread on which the vast majority of the DigiByte discussion occurs. All important updates and news have been released here since the beginning:

- **Bitcointalk**   -https://bitcointalk.org/index.php?topic=408268.0

In essence, the community surrounding and participating in the development of DigiByte is the backbone of the coin. Without a following, the prospects of future adoption and utilisation are starkly limited. DigiByte belongs to all those who use it, not just to the founder who initially created it.

FIRST YEAR HISTORY OF DIGIBYTE

LIST OF CHAPTERS

THE LAUNCH OF DIGIBYTE

JANUARY 2014

I.   Bitcointalk forum thread created for DigiByte.

II.   DigiByte network protocol launched publicly after the pre-mine.

III. Brendon Lindsey interviewed the DigiByte development team.

IV.   DigiByte began to trade on its first cryptocurrency exchange.

V.   Android wallet released, but not initially on the GooglePlay Store.

On the 10th of January 2014 at 07:42:30 UTC, a Bitcointalk thread was created by a user known by the fictitious forum name "DigiByte". This thread was originally titled "[PRE-LAUNCH][DGB] DigiByte—A Professional Crypto Coming". As the title suggests, it had not been launched to the cryptocurrency community yet. In other words, people were not able to mine DigiByte at that time. The first response to this thread was by user "awais3344" five minutes later. He said:

"can you put a countdown timer link? much appreciated"

User "DigiByte" replied within two minutes:

"There is one on the website, but will try and get one on here"

Technically speaking, the first block in the blockchain is called the genesis block. This block showed up as being found on the 10th of January 2014 at 21:13:14 UTC besides a corresponding block reward of zero (some genesis blocks have an attributed reward). Block number one (height one) was successfully found at 22:27:56 UTC on the same day, just over 74 minutes after the genesis block. On the same day, it was announced that user "xtrapool" initiated the first DigiByte mining pool. A bounty of 500,000 DGB was sent to this user for his efforts.

There is sometimes great confusion of the time at which a cryptocurrency launches. With the generation of the first blocks, DigiByte had not publicly launched, but the blockchain had begun. Before the public launch, coins for the pre-mine were being initially mined by the developers. A decision had already been made to distribute half of this pre-mine over the course of several giveaways and promotions. Also, Jared Tate, the founder/creator of DigiByte, posted his first comment on the official DigiByte Bitcointalk thread. On the 11th of January at 19:29:12 UTC, he said:

"I would like to take time to introduce myself as one of the DigiByte developers. I have been active on BitcoinTalk since about this time last year. I have every intention of staying with this coin long-term as this is my first and I plan on being only coin.

A Few Posts I have Made:
A recent Topic I started recently on developing an alt-coin:
https://bitcointalk.org/index.php?topic=389104.0

Vote for DigiByte on a recent poll I started here:
https://bitcointalk.org/index.php?topic=359521.0

And for giggles here is a post I made before the first Bitcoin run up last April. lol:
https://bitcointalk.org/index.php?topic=167611.0"

Below is a visualisation of the first block reward reduction of 77.77%:

Block #1,439 (Reward 72,000) Jan 12th 2014 at 01:04:40 AM UTC

Block #1,440 (Reward 16,000) Jan 12th 2014 at 01:05:11 AM UTC

Also, user "DigiByte" said the wallets for Windows, Mac and Linux will all be available at the launch of the coin.

At block number 1,526, the last coin of the 105,000,000 DGB pre-mine had been mined and so the pre-mine phase of mining had come to an end. Henceforth, it was possible for miners to participate in the mining of DigiByte. Therefore, the official public launch of Digibyte was on the 12th of January 2014 at 17:24:55 UTC at block 1,527 (block reward 16,000 DGB). User "DigiByte" at 19:00:57 UTC said:

"Launched! Still uploading code to git hub!"

About three hours after the public launch of the blockchain, user "DigiByte" gave thanks to all those who had participated. There were very few problems. One problem was due to complications attaining to a certain mining pool called Pick Axe. He reiterated that the development team are in the project for the long term.

Also on the 12th of January at 21:02:18 UTC, an announcement was made that over 10 million DGB had now been given to the community from the giveaway pre-mine wallet address from the initial total of 52.5 million DGB. Two hundred people had received 50,000 each for posting their DGB wallet addresses in a separate designated Bitcointalk thread. This was the end of the first giveaway.

Giveaway address: DFsSa6kVoCyHK8ryZYDNX2fi5294kSuH2Q

On the 13th of January, the first independent online article to discuss DigiByte was written by JP Buntinx. It was titled "DigiByte : A Professionally Transparent Cryptocurrency". He wrote a further three articles based on DigiByte throughout the month of January. Also, Brendon Lindsey also wrote an article at http://www.followthecoin.com/digibyte-launch-first-promising-altcoin-of-2014/

The following displays the last block reduction of January:

Block #5,759 (Reward 16,000) Jan 15th 2014 at 12:45:24 AM UTC

Block #5,760 (Reward 8,000) Jan 15th 2014 at 12:45:37 AM UTC

As the above block illustration shows, the block reward had changed to 8,000 DGB per block at which it would remain for about two years (until DigiShield became active on the 28th of February 2014). Also on the 15th of January, the first DigiByte faucet went live at http://www.digifaucet.com (no longer exists).

By the 16th of January, DigiByte had already been accepted as a method of payment by the following inexhaustive list of merchants:

miniGRAFIK Design: http://minigrafik.com/minigrafik-now-accepting-digibyte-dgb-payment-method/
San Francisco SEO: http://sanfranciscoseoagency.com/cryptocurrency/
Crypto Directory: http://www.cryptodirectory.info/
Glivet Clothing E-Store: http://glivet.com/index.php?
Portuguese Hotel: http://residencialcastor.com.br/
Intraweb Design: http://intrawebstudio.com/contact/
AUSE Electronic Cigarettes: http://ausecigs.com.au/cryptocurrency/
Web911 Creative Agency: http://www.web911.co/
Crypto Crock Alligator Meat: http://cryptocrock.com/

After nearly one week, it was possible to buy development services, clothing, web directory services, hotel rooms and even crocodile meat. A 200,000 DGB bounty was sent to user "WutriCoin" for miniGRAFIK Design as the first merchant to accept DGB as payment method. Also on the 16th of January, Jared Tate was interviewed by Bredon Lindsey (see pages 119 to 125 of the appendix).

On the 17th of January, DigiByte began to trade on its first cryptocurrency exchange called Cryptokopen at http://cryptokopen.eu/digibyte-coin/. The trading pair DGB/EUR was established ready for active trading. This exchange no longer exists. Efforts were being continuously made to get DigiByte added to Cryptsy too.

On the 17th of January at 02:08:18 UTC, two days after DGB were successfully sent from a PC to an Android wallet, user "DigiByte" was quoted as saying:

> "Android Wallet Update:
>
> Thanks to the amazing efforts of xploited the Android wallet looks great and is working! We have sent several transactions back and forth with the QR code reader. We are doing more testing and are working to boost the peer connectivity to make sure that transactions are fast. Just like Google we wont release it until it is fast!
>
> We are also going to activate the QR reader in the Windows, Linux & mac Wallets and re-release them. This will not be a mandatory update as it is only enabling the QR code functionality.
>
> This will be a huge step toward allowing merchants to accept payments from customers smart phones right away at the check out counter."

One day later, another block explorer at http://digitools.pw/chain/DigiByte was created. It no longer exists.

On the 19th of January, the second cryptocurrency exchange called Coin Market began to actively trade DigiByte. It was the first exchange to introduce the DGB/BTC trading pair. In the first 24 hours of trading DGB against BTC, a total trading volume of about 11.63 BTC was recorded according to user "esotericizm". This event was announced on the official DigiByte Bitcointalk thread by user "coinmarket.io" at 21:57:07 UTC:

> "Ladies and gentleman...
>
> DGB has been listed at: https://www.coinmarket.io/market/DGBBTC
>
> there you go!"

Besides the addition to the above exchange on the 19th of January, the first official forum of DigiByte was created by user "WutriCoin" at http://DigiByteTalk.com as well as another block explorer at http://cryptexplorer.com/chain/DigiByte. Unfortunately, both these sites no longer exist.

On the 21st of January, the Android wallet was released. An announcement was made on the official DigiByte Bitcointalk thread by user "DigiByte" at 20:24:50 UTC:

"Alright everyone, we have decided to release the Android Wallet early outside of Google Play! Please report any bugs or issues you may encounter! Thank you to xploited! Please enjoy!

...(DOWNLOAD LINKS)...

Also use http://qrcode.kaywa.com/ to generate QR codes in your wallet until we get the newer wallets released!

You may have to change the settings on your phone to allow for installations outside Google Play. Make sure to back up your wallets!

Make sure to give us some feedback when you try the Android wallet out for the first time! We have tested it on a few different phones, but once we know there is no major issue we will make an announcement on all the social media platforms."

After the above release, an article was written by JP Buntinx titled "DigiByte: Now With Android Wallet". This was the third article he wrote about DigiByte.

On the 23rd of January, an updated Windows wallet client was released. It introduced QR code support into the client and was not mandatory. Updated versions for Mac and Linux were released two days previously. On the same day, user "Giggler" became a DigiByte developer.

Three days after its release, the Android wallet was added to the Google Play Store.

On the 28th of January at 01:52:56 UTC, user "DigiByte" said:

"Keep messaging your favorite exchanges! Also bump this thread if it falls to the second page. It make a huge difference in traffic and new users when people find this thread on the first page. Many people are looking for a sold coin to get behind and are overwhelemed with the crypto world right now. Lets give them a solid foundation to start from! Also we will be giving out random bounties to people posting pictures with supportive or funny sayings encouraging the adoption of DigiByte! We are still working hard behind the scenes for all of you!"

On the 29th of January, Cryptorush began to trade DigiByte. User "DigiByte" at 03:17:10 UTC on the 30th of January said:

> "Make sure to check out DigiByte on the new exchange Crypto Rush!
> https://cryptorush.in/"

On the penultimate day of January, a dev team update was posted on Bitcointalk. It notified the community that work was being done on user tutorials, promotional videos and website modifications. After the addition of a few more exchanges, further progress would then begin on marketing the coin in order to attract more users. One idea was to take advantage of the Facebook advertisement service.

Other events which occurred in the month of January were:

- A Facebook group was created on the 10th of January.

- A Twitter page (@DigiByte2) was created on the 12th of January.

- On the 12th of January at 18:39:10 UTC, the DigiByte Subreddit was created at www.reddit.com/r/Digibyte.

- On the 13th of January, the first block explorer for DGB was made available at the website http://altexplorer.net.

- A discussion took place in the middle of the month about changing from DGB to DIGI. It remained as DGB after a community vote had occurred.

- On the 21st of January, the slogan "You store data in megabytes and gigabytes, why not send money in DigiBytes" slogan was born.

- Development began on an exchange specifically for DigiByte on the 29th of January. A platform similar to BitPay and Coinbase was sought after as a means to have a direct DGB to fiat currency (USD) option.

- On the last day of the month, DigiByte was added to the Cryptsy exchange wikipedia page at http://wiki.cryptsy.com/dgb.

DIGISHIELD VERSION 2.0 WALLET CLIENT RELEASED

FEBRUARY 2014

I.   DigiByte official mascot created by "bman3".

II.   All time high market capitalisation of 2014 reached.

III.   DigiByte began to trade on four cryptocurrency exchanges.

IV.   DigiByte version 2.0.0 wallet client released called DigiShield.

V.   Block reward reduced from 8,000 DGB to 7,960 DGB per block.

About three weeks had passed since the first block was verified and added to the DigiByte blockchain. Since that time, the coin had achieved the following:

* Over 10,000 wallet downloads.

* About 50,000 hits on the official website.

* A functioning Windows, Mac, Linux & Android wallet with QR code support.

The development team were also happy to reiterate current projects being worked upon. Some of these were:

* A professional promotional video and "how-to" tutorial guides.

* Updates to the official website (appearance, functionality and servers).

* DigiByte's very own exchange and foundation.

On the first day of February, user "bman3" published his own individual designs of a DigiByte mascot. A post was submitted by user "DigiByte" at 21:52:06 UTC on the same day. He said:

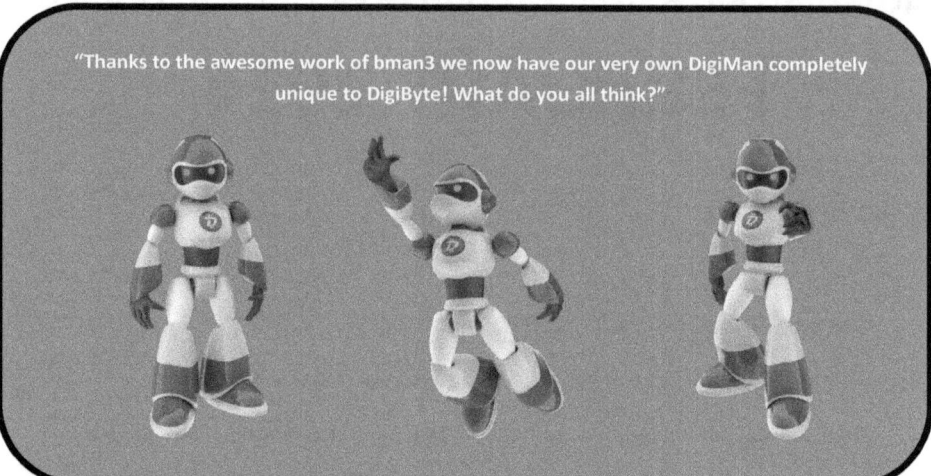

"Thanks to the awesome work of bman3 we now have our very own DigiMan completely unique to DigiByte! What do you all think?"

Two responses to these designs were:

"martins"
"holy Mofo's thats an awesome robot there!!! Strenght and security it's what i see."

"Triax"
"looks good except he doesnt look very friendly and helpful. which is needed. he looks angry and like he is going to beat the crap out of you if you get it wrong, just need to change the top brow shape"

On the 4th of February, there was concern why DigiByte had not yet been added to the exchange called Cryptsy. User "DigiByte" at 18:29:12 UTC said:

"We do not understand it either. We are more than willing to help get DigiByte on an exchange in any way we can. We have sent them messages but have heard no reply.

Does anyone know of a direct support email or email to get a hold of Big Vern?
And if anyone from Cryptsy reads this please PM the DigiByte account.
We are very interested in having DigiByte get listed on Cryptsy."

Shortly after the mascot designs were published, constructive criticism was given to "bman3". DigiMan's eye brows were altered in order to make him look friendly. On the 5th of February at 05:05:07 UTC, user "DigiByte" was quoted as saying:

"Bman3 has made some tweaks to the DigiMan and is making a few more.
We think he looks great! What do you all think?"

Three responses to these modifications were:

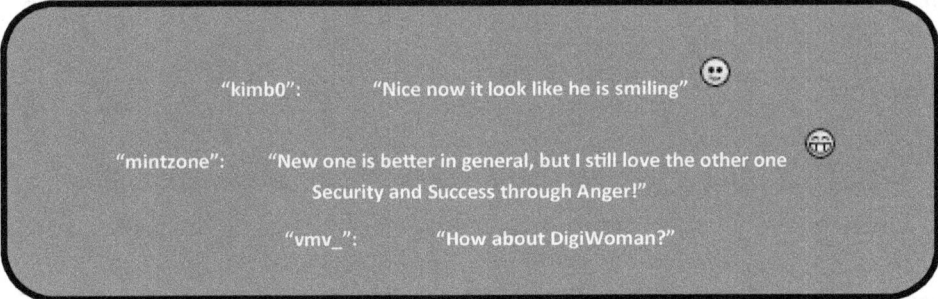

"kimb0": "Nice now it look like he is smiling"

"mintzone": "New one is better in general, but I still love the other one
Security and Success through Anger!"

"vmv_": "How about DigiWoman?"

Also on the 5th of February, DigiByte began active trading on the exchange called CryptX.io. It was the fourth exchange addition. It has since closed down.

On the following day, the website www.coinmarketcap.com incorporated DigiByte into its list of cryptocurrencies. It ranks the calculated market capitalisations of hundreds of coins based on their average fiat price from an array of exchanges and their respective total generated coins. It also displays the total daily trading volume of the last 24 hours of each coin besides other statistics. DigiByte was initially listed at number 44 on the site.

Also on the 6th of February:

- The trading pair DGB/BTC was initiated on the Coined Up exchange.

- An all time high market capitalisation of about $641,000 was reached for the year 2014. At this peak, it was worth 0.01 mBTC per unit of DGB account according to Coined Up.

On the 9th of February, several designs of paper wallets were submitted by forum members of Bitcointalk. User "xploited" gave designers DGB as a reward for these:

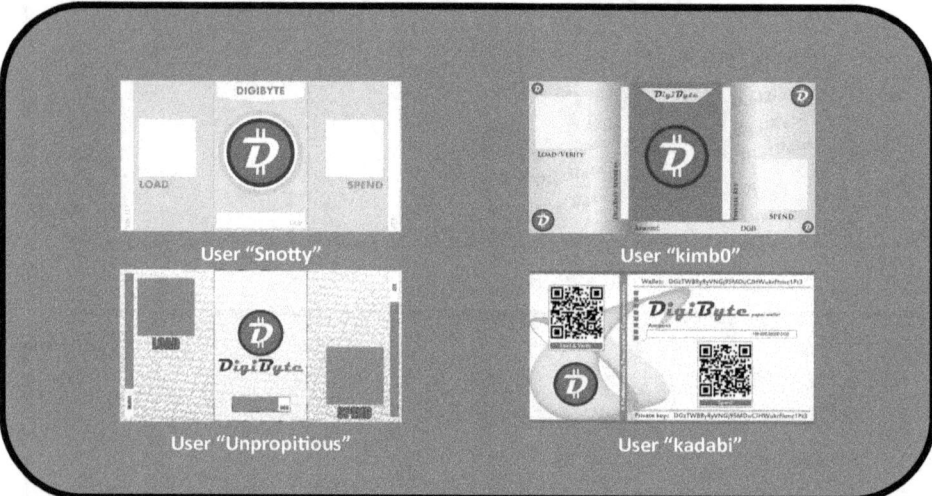

On the 12th of February, MintPal began to trade DigiByte against Bitcoin on their exchange platform. On their official Twitter page, the following was tweeted:

"The DigiByte and microCoin BTC markets are now live. Happy trading!

http://www.mintpal.com/market/DGB/BTC/"

MintPal launched on the 5th of February (one week earlier) and registered a total first day volume of just over 60 BTC. The DigiByte development team donated 0.10985853 BTC in order to help the coin achieve top spot on the MintPal voting list just before the addition. They wanted to get on as many exchanges as possible.

On the 13th of February at 20:58:24 UTC, user "DigiByte" made an announcement regarding an invitation to attend an upcoming scheduled conference:

"So the DigiByte "creator" has just received an invitation to speak at the upcoming Crypto Convention on April 9th in New York at the Midtown Manhattan Hilton.

@DigiByteCoin @DigibyteNews
How can we connect with lead team or Creator of #digibyte
Want them to speak at http://www.CryptoCurrencyConvention.com RT

I Jared (BitcoinTate) as the creator/founder would be honored to attend and speak on behalf DigiByte. I will be releasing my LinkedIn profile in the coming days and plan on becoming transparent with exactly who I am.
I am proud of DigiByte and I am very committed to its future.

Not sure what all the convention will entail, but I am looking forward to finding out more about it. I feel this will be a great opportunity to help show DigiByte to the world and to network with fellow crypto enthusiasts."

Five days later, user "r3wt" at 00:06:31 UTC notified the community of the latest exchange to add DigiByte. He posted the following comment:

"added DGB to openex. https://openex.pw/index.php?page=trade&market=115"

About two minutes later, user "DigiByte" responded:

"This is awesome! Thank you very much!"

On the same day, a decision was made by the developers to change the block reward reduction schedule. From a certain future date/block number (both yet to be specified), the reward per block would reduce 0.5% every 10,108 blocks (each week) beginning from the current 8,000 DGB reward.

After successful tests of the new block reduction and difficulty re-targeting code had been made on testnet, an announcement was made by user "DigiByte". On the 23rd of February at 21:48:39 UTC, he posted the following:

> ### "DigiByte v2.0 DigiShield has been released!!
>
> 1) Make sure to back up your wallet.dat as always! File -> Back Up Wallet - > Save!
>
> 2) Git Source, Windows, Mac OSX and Ubuntu released. Android coming shortly.
>
> 3) qrc_bitcoin.cpp & digibyte-qt.exe are the only two files that need to be replaced for the Windows Wallet in main install folder!
> Just swap out files, no changes needed to app data folders. Or download and replace entire DigiByte install folder. Executable download coming soon as well for Windows.
>
> ### ...(DOWNLOAD LINKS)...
>
> Android coming shortly.
> Pool owners PM us when you have updated! All pools will be listed with a line crossing them in red until they have updated starting tomorrow! Thanks for your patience!
>
> ### Update must be made by next Friday @ block 67200!"

Cryptocurrency exchanges and mining pools were contacted in order to notify them of this mandatory update and future hard fork in the blockchain. They had to send the development team a private message to confirm they had updated to v2.0.

On the 24th of February, "DigiByte" responded to the comment "What happens if I do not update my wallet?". His answer was:

> "Your wallet could reject the block chain once the hard fork occurs at block 67200. Also, you can experience problems sending & receiving coins. This is why the update is "Mandatory."
>
> By changing the the block reward and difficulty adjustment code we had no choice but to "fork" the DigiByte blockchain."

On the 27th of February, there was confirmation that Coined Up, Cryptorush and MintPal had updated to DigiShield. On the other hand, there was no response on whether Coin Market had updated. In addition, the community were encouraged to make sure mining pools knew they had to update to the new version.

On the next day, a few mining pools and Coin Market were removed from official lists on the DigiByte official website and Bitcointalk thread. The development team encouraged the community to support those sites that had updated.

> Block #67,199 (Reward 8,000) Feb 28th 2014 at 10:50:50 PM UTC

> Block #67,200 (Reward 7,960) Feb 28th 2014 at 10:52:17 PM UTC

Before the generation of block number 67,200, a total of 664,248,000 DGB had been mined. The block reward would continue to reduce by 0.5% every 10,800 blocks from that block. In addition to this, the difficulty re-targeting time changed from 144 minutes (2.4 hours) to 60 seconds (DigiShield).

Other events which occurred in the month of February were:

- The first known real transaction in DGB for goods/services took place at the Residencial Castor Hotel Inn in Brazil.

- AllCrypt introduced DigiByte to their voting list on the 4th of February.

- On the 6th of February, the total number of views of the official DigiByte Bitcointalk thread surpassed 100,000.

- Five hours before block number 67,200, an updated Android wallet was uploaded to the Google Play Store.

DIGIBYTE BEGAN TO TRADE ON SEVEN
EXCHANGES INCLUDING CRYPTSY

MARCH 2014

I.   DigiShield implemented into the Dogecoin network protocol.

II.   DigiByte began trading on the exchange called Cryptsy.

III.   DigiByte added to a further six cryptocurrency exchanges.

IV.   DigiByte version 2.9.0 wallet client released

V.   Preparations made for the upcoming New York City Crypto Convention.

Sixty eight minutes had passed since the new difficulty re-targeting algorithm (DigiShield) became active. Instead of the difficulty of mining changing every 144 minutes, it would now change after each and every block (60 seconds).

The main reason why the developers implemented DigiShield was in order to protect the network protocol from abuse from multi-pools. It is known that when the difficulty is low and takes a long time to re-target, a coin can be mined quickly and easily before the difficulty increases to counteract a surge in hashing power. Once the difficulty re-targets to a higher number, hashing power can leave the multi-pool, which leaves the network in a state of low hash and high difficulty. This inevitably leads to bloated block times and fewer coins being mined. Therefore, the purpose of DigiShield is to allow the difficulty of mining to fluctuate almost perfectly in sync with changes in the net hash processing power committed by miners towards finding blocks.

Fifty different difficulty re-targeting algorithms were tested over a five day period in order to produce the code of DigiShield. It outperformed all the other ones.

On the 3rd of March at 17:07:41 UTC, user "DigiByte" was quoted as saying:

> "Some people have expressed an opinion that the difficulty is changing to much or too fast. That is what it is supposed to do when the net hash changes up or down.
>
> The difference is no other coin difficulty changes and adapts as quick as DigiShield. It is about as instant as you can get. It is much more accurate at mirroring the actuall hash rate than any other system including Kimoto Gravity Well. Even with the Kimoto Gravity Well Multipools still have the chance to "instamine" for quite a few blocks when they jump on a coin. Then one they leave the KMG can get "Stuck" for awhile at a higher difficulty.
>
> We saw a sudden increase from less than 2 GH to over 8 GH yesterday. DigiShield performed beautifully and the multipools got a very small amount of coins compared to what they are used to getting. Not only that, but we never were "Stuck" at a high difficulty like most other coins would have been with such a dramatic increase in hash."

A couple of days later, the development team spent 2 BTC ($1,500 at the time) equivalent of the pre-mine as a means to help get DigiByte added to Cryptsy. To be specific, votes were bought in order to push the coin up the list of potential coins to be added to this exchange. The development team thought this was sufficient to cover the expense of adding DigiByte by Cryptsy. Besides this, many supporters of the coin were regularly voting for free or buying further votes.

User "DigiByte" also called Cryptsy via telephone to discuss the addition. It was later on the 5th of March that DigiByte reached number one spot on the voting list.

Other exchanges looked upon as favourable were Bter and BTC38 in China.

The first block reduction since block number 67,200 (DigiShield began) took place:

Block #77,279 (Reward 7,960) Mar 10th 2014 at 02:38:25 PM UTC

Block #77,280 (Reward 7,920.2) Mar 10th 2014 at 02:40:18 PM UTC

Due to the success of DigiShield, other cryptocurrencies had begun to show interest. In particular, discussions were being held with the developers of Dogecoin who ultimately adopted and implemented the algorithm into their network protocol on the 12th of March. As a favour, the Dogecoin community helped vote for DigiByte on Cryptsy's list of potential coin additions.

On the 14th of March, user "torchwood-uk" posted an announcement for the community on the official DigiByte Bitcointalk thread at 13:28:26 UTC:

"BigVern @cryptsy

The following new markets have been added:
DGB/BTC, SAT/BTC, RDD/BTC, ZED/BTC"

Cryptsy is a cryptocurrency trading exchange launched on the 20th of May 2013 and based in Delray Beach, Florida, USA. It has become one of the most reputable and respected exchanges. At the time of publication of this book, it is still active.

Three other exchanges added DigiByte to their platforms on or before the 14th of March. These were (date they began active trading in brackets) the following:

Comkort (02/03/2014)	It opened for beta testing on the 20th of February 2014 and went live on the 1st of March 2014. Based in Estonia, it closed on the 20th of July 2015.
AllCrypt (04/03/2014)	Announced on the 29th of January 2014, users were able to register and vote for their favourite coin from the 4th of February. No longer active.
Swisscex (14/03/2014)	Based in Switzerland, it went active on the 1st of February 2014. It was established in January 2014, but is no longer active.

Block #87,359 (Reward 7,960) Mar 22nd 2014 at 08:35:46 AM UTC

Block #87,360 (Reward 7,880.599) Mar 22nd 2014 at 08:37:21 AM UTC

Discussions were held as to whether the term "currency" should be dropped from all publications and promotions. A clearer description of what DigiByte is was sought after. One suggestion (now widely adopted by the community) was posted by "DigiByte" on the 26th of March:

"DigiByte is a decentralized crypto payment network based upon Litecoin & Bitcoin that works similar to PayPal & Western Union. DigiByte is fast, secure & world-wide!"

On the 28th of March at 06:09:36 UTC, user "DigiByte" said:

"We understand everyone's urgency to change the algo right away. But this is something we cannot simply do over night. We still have a few months before this becomes an issue. We agree we want to be proactive. But we also do not want to mess up the existing DigiByte infrastructure.

Before we replace the main download link on the website we wanted to release DigiByte v2.9 on here to get a few more testers feedback. We have tested it out and everything appears to be working well.

DigiByte v 2.9 Facts:
*It is not a mandatory update
*Backwords compatible
*Includes exe installer
*Implements the latest Bitcoin 0.9 protocol features into DigiByte.

...(DOWNLOAD LINKS)...

As always BACK UP your wallet.dat before upgrading!"

Before the end of March, a further three exchanges had begun trading DigiByte (see the table below). Prelude by Moolah was the first exchange to offer direct DGB/USD trading from the 22nd of March, one week after trading started there.

AGX.io (15/03/2014)	It was announced in early February 2014 on Bitcointalk. Users were able to register from the 27th of February 2014. It went live on the 15th of March.
Prelude (15/03/2014)	
Cryptokk (20/03/2014)	It went live on the 11th of March 2014. Ten cryptocurrencies were initially available at the beginning. It no longer exists.

Attention at the end of the month was primarily focused on the upcoming Cryptocurrency Convention in New York City on the 9th of April. Jared Tate was looking forward to giving a speech to an audience of potential investors, media and cryptocurrency fans. It would be a great opportunity to make more people aware of DigiByte. Work was being done to produce the relevant presentational and marketing materials for the speech.

Other events which occurred in the month of March were:

- On the 14th of March, www.digiaddress.org went live thanks to user "xploited". It was a site used to generate and print paper wallets.

- On the 14th of March, notice was given by user "r3wt" for OpenEx (exchange) users to withdraw their DigiByte by the 27th of March 2014.

- On the 20th of March, 1,000 DGB were sent to the 1,000th Twitter follower.

- Over 30 million transactions had taken place on the DigiByte network by the 25th of March.

- On the 26th of March, Cryptorush (an exchange) was removed from all official links and promotional material by user "DigiByte".

- A fundraiser was initiated on the 30th of March to help the victims of the Oso, Washington, United States mudslide on the 22nd of March.

NEW YORK CITY CRYPTOCURRENCY CONVENTION
APRIL 2014

I.   Cryptocurrency Convention in New York City at the Scholastic Auditorium.

II.   "Digi-Awareness Campaign" began.

III.   DigiByte collaborated with Brian Kelly from CNBC.

IV.   Version 2.9.1 of the Windows and Linux wallet client officially released.

V.   "How to Upgrade your Windows Wallet to v2.9.1" video uploaded.

On the first day of April, user "DigiByte" published the promotional material to be used on the 9th of April. At 01:10:30 UTC, he posted the comment:

An additional final version of the DigiByte Pop-Up Banner for the Cryptocurrency Convention in New York City was also published on the same day (size approx. 6 foot tall, 34 inch wide (see page 58 on the right)).

Block #97,439 (Reward 7,880.599) Apr 2nd 2014 at 11:13:32 PM UTC

Block #97,440 (Reward 7,841.196005) Apr 2nd 2014 at 11:13:38 PM UTC

On the 3rd of April, user "DigiByte" at 01:47:40 UTC was quoted as saying:

"We wanted to give everyone an update on the potential algorithm change. While we are still focusing on gearing up for the Crypto Currency convention next week we are planning on doing several tests with a multi-algorithm implementation in the next couple weeks."

About four hours later, user "amdfxman1701" was quoted as saying:

"I agree! Ya'll are doing a great job. Only a handful of other coins have devs as dedicated as ya'll. For that reason alone, I believe Digibyte has a bright 2014-2015.

Can't wait!"

Another user called "Th3P" also commented:

"Good to hear, Really hope the convention goes well."

On the 7th of April, DigiByte began to trade on the cryptocurrency exchange called EuropEx at https://www.europex.eu/#coin/btc/dgb. However, it closed its doors on the 14th of July 2015 due to server problems. "Europex brings crypto-coins in Europe" was the slogan used by EuropEx.

On the 9th of April, the day of the Cryptocurrency Convention in New York City at the Scholastic Auditorium had arrived. Jared Tate gave a speech about DigiByte as well as answering a few questions. On the official DigiByte Bitcointalk thread at 18:24:30 UTC, user "oranges411" posted the following from the event:

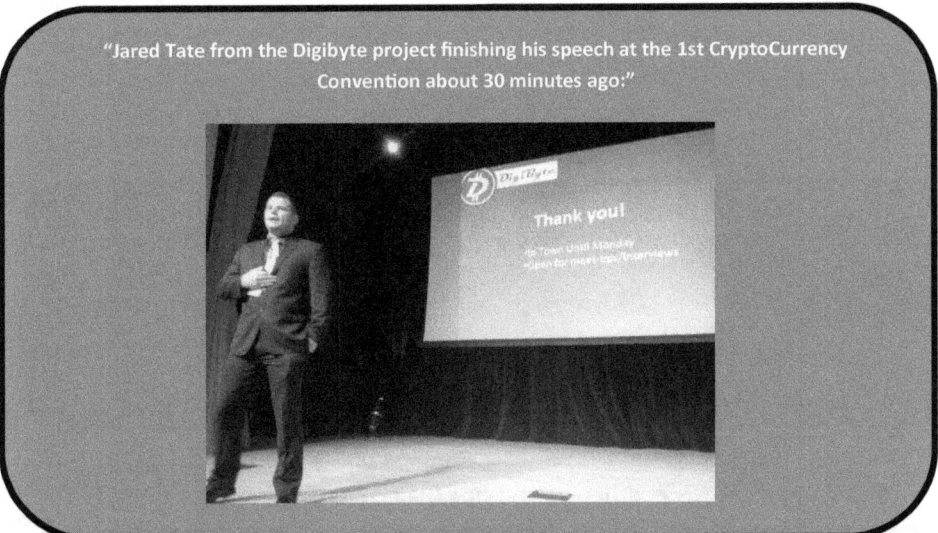

"Jared Tate from the Digibyte project finishing his speech at the 1st CryptoCurrency Convention about 30 minutes ago:"

User "DigiByte" gave feedback regarding the speech and reception:

"The convention went very well! DigiByte was very well received and we have made several awesome connections. Including some wall street financial firms! We are meeting up with more people later tonight at the New York Bitcoin center for an after party. We will post more feedback later tonight or tomorrow."

Five days later, the DigiByte team travelled back from New York City. A full video of Jared Tate's speech was uploaded to YouTube one week later (21st of April).

Block #107,519 (Reward 7,841.196005) Apr 15th 2014 at 12:17:20 PM UTC

Block #107,520 (Reward 7,801.990025) Apr 15th 2014 at 12:22:29 PM UTC

On the 15th of April, CryptoCzar became the second exchange of the month to begin trading DigiByte. Jared Tate had personally met its founders at the convention in New York City. It no longer exists. They were described as a U.S. based FinCEN registered cryptocurrency exchange.

A key milestone concerning the blockchain occurred on the 18th of April. It was the generation of a cumulative total of just over one billion DGB since block number one. This occurred at block number 109,725 at 11:21:29 UTC.

One day later at 19:29:25 UTC, user "DigiByte" made the following announcement:

> "We are very excited to announce we will be working with Brian Kelly from CNBC's Fast Money to help improve his coin NautilusCoin that he launched on CNBC!
>
> He will also be helping us Promote DigiByte in exchange for our help!
>
> Here is a video of the launch: http://www.cnbc.com/id/101573131"

On the same day, a social media teaser video was uploaded to YouTube. It is an animated video seven seconds long displaying the active social media sites of DGB:

> www.DigiByte.co
> www.twitter.com/DigiByteCoin
> www.facebook.com/DigiByteCoin
> www.youtube.com/DigiByteCoin

In the last week of the month, the development team were working around the clock to update several things. They were also getting ready to help Brian Kelly from CNBC launch Nautiluscoin. It was launched on the 29th of April 2014. One notable part of the coin's specification was the implementation of DigiShield.

> Block #117,599 (Reward 7,801.990025) Apr 29th 2014 08:55:52 PM at UTC

> Block #117,600 (Reward 7,762.980075) Apr 29th 2014 at 08:56:29 PM UTC

On the last day of the month, user "DigiByte" at 12:09:33 UTC posted:

"DigiByte version 2.9.1 has officially been launched! We are using the launch to kick off our DigiByte Beginner Guide video series with a video guide to help you upgrade your Windows DigiByte wallet!

View the video here and make sure to subscribe to our YouTube channel to get all the newest video releases.
https://www.youtube.com/watch?v=-Yr8fdwhx2Y&feature=youtu.be

We will be featuring a Beginner, Mining, Trading and Merchant series of videos. There will also be a Founders Fire Side Chat series where Jared will talk about several issues facing DigiByte and the current state of the crypto economy.

This launch also coincides with the creation of a news & press release section on the DigiByte website where this will be posted.

More news and announcements to come concerning an algorithm change, investors and media attention!
...(DOWNLOAD LINKS)...
Mac OSX wallet has been built but we are working on packaging it for deployment. It will be available soon. We are also working on releasing a media kit for promotional purposes that everyone can use."

Also on this day, a video was uploaded to YouTube titled "How to upgrade your Windows DigiByte Wallet to v2.9.1". The video features Jared Tate who goes through the necessary steps for users to follow:

https://www.youtube.com/watch?v=-Yr8fdwhx2Y&feature=youtu.be

Other events which occurred in the month of April were:

- On the 15th of April, user "DigiByte" felt proof of stake (PoS) would be counter productive for the long term sustained growth of DigiByte.

- On the 24th of April, another article was written by JP Buntinx titled "DigiByte Revisited : DigiShield, NYC Convention Video, And Much More!"

ANNOUNCEMENT OF THE CHANGE TO MULTI-ALGO

MAY 2014

I.   DigiByte mentioned live on CNBC.

II.   DigiByte Tipbot goes live on Reddit (10,000 giveaway).

III.   DigiByte version 2.9.1 Mac wallet client released.

IV.   Jared's continuous 24/7 effort to get DigiByte mainstream.

V.   YouTube video detailed the future algorithm change to Multi-Algo.

On the first day of the month, an article was published by Brian Kelly (@BKBrianKelly) on www.cnbc.com titled "How I'm dodging bitcoin's flaw". He is the founder and managing member of Brian Kelly Capital LLC. In the article, he made reference to the recently developed and implemented re-targeting algorithm called DigiShield. After seeing how successful it had been for DigiByte, he chose to implement the code into his own created cryptocurrency called Nautiluscoin.

On the following day, DigiByte was mentioned live on CNBC's finance segment "Fast Money" with Brian Kelly at 17:00 ET.

Also at the beginning of the month, a downloadable media kit was made available on the official DigiByte website in order to further promote the coin. Its purpose is to inform those who wish to describe and explain DigiByte to an audience.

A significant increase in the Bitcoin Satoshi price of one unit of DigiByte account occurred in the last few days of April and into May. By the 1st of May, the price had more than doubled in about three days. Two popular exchanges at the time were Cryptsy and MintPal. According to the site www.cryptocoincharts.info, the values from these two exchanges were:

	Price on Cryptsy	Price on MintPal	Volume on Cryptsy	Volume on Mintpal
	(BTC Satoshi)	(BTC Satoshi)	(BTC)	(BTC)
28th of April	30	30.5	3.34789	1.70551
29th of April	39.5	41	11.6774	38.1962
30th of April	60.5	65	40.4676	62.0228
1st of May	65.5	72.5	29.2970	71.5445
2nd of May	65.5	66.5	7.89045	14.5705

On the 8th of May, the DigiByte TipBot went live (/u/dgbTipBot) on Reddit. A 10,000 DGB giveaway occurred in order to celebrate it.

On the following day, UltraCoin creator Reggie Middleton and Brian Kelly of Brian Kelly Capital discussed some of the alternatives to Bitcoin live on CNBC at about 14:40 ET. Brian Kelly was quoted as saying "There's another one called DigiByte which is actually a pretty serious competitor to PayPal I think, at least to the system payment area. They've got a great development team." The full video can be found at http://video.cnbc.com/gallery/?video=3000274165.

On the 10th of May at 22:46:46 UTC, user "DigiByte" assured the community that progress was being made. He was quoted as saying:

"We are working on some things to completely separate us from the pack.

We apologize for not being very active these past few days but we are working to get some important things done to push us to the top."

Four days later at 23:44:32 UTC, user "DigiByte" announced the new Mac OS X v2.9.1 wallet client:

"After countless hours of frustration, we have finally compiled a v2.9.1 OSX DMG installer that should work for everyone! We could use some more testers!
Please let us know if you were able to install this version on your Mac!"

http://www.digibyte.co/sites/digibyte.co/files//crypto/DigiByte-Qt-v2.9.1-OSX.dmg

In the middle of the month, members of the community were asking for frequent progress updates from the development team. There were some people who thought not much was happening. Some of their concerns were:

- To change the algorithm so that less heat is generated during mining.

- To make sure the security of the DGB network protocol takes high priority.

- To possibly alter the number of total coins of 21 billion in 21 years.

Block # 127,679 (Reward 7,762.980075) May 20th 2014 at 11:39:20 PM UTC

Block #127,680 (Reward 7,724.165174) May 20th 2014 at 11:39:26 PM UTC

About 1,139,691,008 DGB had been mined up to and including block number 127,679.

On the 23rd of May at 17:14:06 UTC, user "DigiByte" posted an announcement from Jared Tate concerning his recent activity and future news. He said:

"Greetings Everyone,

Just wanted to give you all a quick update to let you know we are still here and working. I (Jared) have had some personal issues arise the past couple weeks I have had to deal with. Including a move to a new location which required me to move the filming studio I had set up. We have just about set up a new one so we can begin rolling out videos once more.

I personally have been working on DigiByte since the beginning of last December pretty much 7 days a week non stop. Some times 14+ hours a day. So I have neglected other parts of my life which I am now paying for. I have now got those issues sorted out and I am working with others on the team (who still have full time jobs) to keep working on future developments.

We have been talking with some serious investors the past couple weeks at least every other day. We will be flying to LA on June 2nd to hopefully finalize a deal. This process has been very time consuming as it has required some very detailed plans and research to be done as to how we can properly build & market an exchange in todays uncertain regulatory environment.

With recent developments that have arisen in the algorithm aspect of cryptos we have held of on officially announcing an algo change until we know for sure we are making the right move.

We apologize if we have not responded to some people yet but we have received countless messages from other coins asking us to implement DigiShield into their coin with zero to little compensation for our time or energy. We definitely want to support the development of crypto currency technology but we only have some many hours in the day and limited financial resources at the moment.

Stay tuned for more info and feel free to help us out how ever you think you can and we are very much looking toward the future! You guys rock as a community!

- Jared

On the 23rd of May at 17:26:56 UTC, user "wegsturm" said:

> "Thank you and your team for your hard work!
> I know how it is if you neglect private life in favor of work. Hopefully the people around have enough understanding how important this period is in your life.
>
> If it would be easy to have success, everyone would be successfull.
> You never get something for free that is worth fighting for!"

On the 31st of May at 17:27:08 UTC, an important announcement was made by user "DigiByte". On the DigiByte Bitcointalk forum thread, he was quoted as saying:

> "DigiByte is officially going to change algorithms!
> We are also meeting with investors this weekend!"
>
> https://www.youtube.com/watch?v=r-0T99DZmI4

In the uploaded video titled "DigiByte Algorithm Change & Status Update: 5/31/14", Jared Tate began by personally thanking the DigiByte community for supporting the continuous development of the coin. The new algorithm would be based on the one used in Myriadcoin together with some incorporated innovation from the DGB developers. This new hashing algorithm would consist of five separate algorithms, hence the name Multi-Algo. Other details announced were:

- SHA-256 and Scrypt had already been chosen.

- Three other GPU friendly algorithms to still choose (easy to mine so to make mining more accessible and more decentralised)

- He said the new mining algorithm would be implemented in a few months time, but no specific date had been set. He made it clear that the algorithm would be tested thoroughly and made sure to properly work before its implementation.

- He invited the community to help test it when ready.

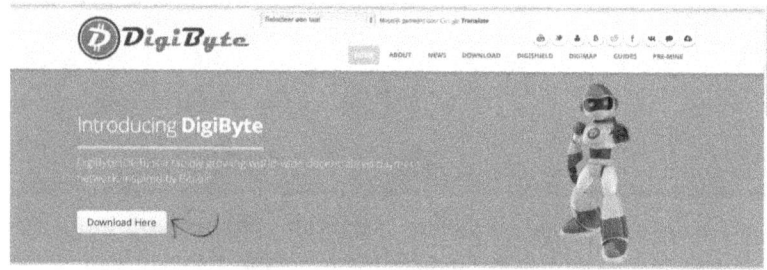

DigiByte A Decentralized Payment Network

(ABOVE) Official DigiByte Website Homepage in June 2014

TESTING OF MULTI-ALGO BEGAN

JUNE 2014

I.   Jared Tate travelled to Los Angeles to meet potential investors.

II.   Bloated block times due to very low mining processing power (hash).

III. Initial testing began on a compiled Multi-Algo qt wallet client.

IV.   Official DigiByte website interface image changed.

V.   Development team attended the "Inside Bitcoins" conference in Hong Kong.

Some people wanted the new algorithm implemented straight away. User "DigiByte" at 19:38:06 UTC on the last day of the previous month said:

> "To those wanting an instant algo change. That is not realistic or possible."

On the 1st of June, user "RJF" at 13:58:25 UTC posted the following reply:

> "Well said. A very wise, and rich, stock market investor once told me the real investment is patience, the money is just a way of showing that you have invested enough patience to make a profit down the road. This has worked for me more often than not over the years. I'll hold, and buy, and mine and wait. That's the way of things invested.
>
> Great job devs, keep up the excellent PR, it can also make or break a coin..."

Simply put, the development team emphasised their commitment towards taking their time with future updates. This was especially the case with the future Multi-Algo update. All newly developed code henceforth would be tested thoroughly with help from the community. This would reduce the risk of (not eliminate) any flaws or bugs in the final release.

Also in the first few days of June, the development team visited Los Angeles to meet potential investors. They were working on a deal to get DigiByte accepted in 1,000+ physical retail stores. A lot of effort was being made to promote the coin.

On the 3rd of June at 22:05:28 UTC, user "DigiByte" said:

> "We are working on multiple fronts right now. The Crypto mining community is tiny compared to the potential consumer base we could be looking at here. The point is we are working to gain very serious attention for DigiByte on multiple fronts. We want mining to be fair. But if we gain merchants on a larger scale than Bitcoin and especially litecoin an algo change may not be possible or necessary. But as of right now it is still the plan."

On the same day, it was evident the DigiByte network protocol had been struggling over the past several weeks. Blocks were taking a very long time to generate. On the 4th of June at 09:35:53 UTC, user "DigiByte" was quoted as saying:

> "DigiByte has now become a victim of its own success. Despite our integrity, our transparency and our contributions to the entire crypto currency community there are those who wish to maliciously attack us for their own person gain.
>
> The current block times with multipools are a testimate to that.
> Had this happened to another coin or Bitcoin in the same proportions months could pass before the next block is found.
>
> Crypto currency is an ever evolving market and field that is changing at an unprecedented pace. We will continue to adapt, improvise and overcome.
>
> They key is to keep things in perspective. We see the light at the end of the tunnel. A brighter future will emerge for all of us.
> We can stand and work together or we can hang seperatly."

The network protocol hash rate (the overall processing power committed by miners in order to successfully find blocks) had been fluctuating wildly. This had been the case since the 28th of April (two months after DigiShield became operational).

In order to resolve this problem, more hash would be required. Alternatively, if need be, an update to the code could be released. The developers thought that releasing an update (hard fork) before the Multi-Algo update would be counter productive, so they chose to focus on encouraging the community to add extra hash to the network.

On the 10th of June at 15:38:11 UTC, user "DigiByte" said:

"Yes, we have the same thing on our machines.
When the next block is discovered it will sync.
It says it is trying to sync with the network in the mean time.

Our network hash rate has dropped to the lowest point it has ever been since launch.
DigiShield is still working but it needs to be adjusted with such a low hash rate.
Something in the new 0.9.1 code is causing it to average out at a much
higher difficulty than it should.

We are working hard on getting the multi-algo ready to go. In the mean time we are
prepping to rent some more hash for a few days at a loss.
Please be patient and understand DigiByte is not going anywhere.

If you look at all the other Scrypt coins their hash is the lowest they have been as well.
It is like almost overnight GPU miners have left Scrypt all together."

A couple of minutes later on, he also said:

"At this point it does not appear to be an attack.
We have seen a large drop in hash recently and the difficulty is averaging previous blocks
still much more than it should. This would kill other coins off. If it happened to Bitcoin it
could take weeks before the next block would be found."

On the 12th of June at 00:06:22 UTC, user "DigiByte" said:

> "We are going to make mining for everyone as fair as possible as well as making sure the block timing returns to normal.
> We are working on compiling the new wallets for testnet right now.
> There will be a lot of changes to the code base.
> We are trying to do in a week what we planned on would take us a couple months. But it is our #1 priority right now."

There were some people on the official DigiByte Bitcointalk forum who were trying their best to misinform, attack or discredit the coin. On the 15th of June at 01:28:02 UTC, user "DigiByte" said:

> "You can think what you like. If you you do not want to be involved with DigiByte please leave and stop spreading FUD. We do not want community members who are constantly complaining and throwing around unfounded accusations in an immature manner.
> If you want instant gratification there are plenty of pump & dumps to go get involved with right now and other threads where you will fit right in with your pointless comments.
>
> Why not try helping by contributing to the future of DigiByte? This is an OPEN SOURCE project so if you are personally gaining from DigiByte why not help make it better instead of wasting everyone's time?
>
> We are working very hard and we have been transparent since day one. We have been committed to our long term vision and will continue to do so. We are moving forward with a plan and as any
> reasonable person would understand, sometimes things don't always go exactly as planned.
>
> Good news is we have now have the multi-algo code compiled into a QT and we have started testing."

On the following day, the development team had definitely decided which four (out of five) algorithms to include in Multi-Algo. Groestl, SHA-256, Scrypt and Qubit (best CPU algo 3:1 GPU:CPU) were chosen. Groestl was praised as the most energy efficient mining algorithm. A conversation was already taking place about the fifth algorithm to be included.

They were happy to announce that Multi-Algo mining will dramatically reduce the chance of a 51% attack on the network protocol. It would also result in fairer mining. An attacker would need control three out of five algorithms in order to conduct a 51% attack.

Multi-Algo would be equally split and weighted between the five different singular hashing algorithms. Each algorithm would have its own independent difficulty. It would put SHA ASICs at the same level as GPU, Scrypt ASIC and CPU miners.

On the 20th of June at 06:47:02 UTC, user "DigiByte" said:

> "We have successfully tested a DigiByte algorithm switch at a specific block & mined blocks on all 5 algorithms!"

Four minutes later, user "CryptoLTD" said:

> "Awesome! Forward progression!"

Other events which occurred in June were:

- Work began on a DGB iPhone App on the 4th of June. Apple had permitted the development of crypto apps. Help was welcomed to develop it.

- DigiByte was added to Poloniex's voting list of future potential coin additions on the 13th of June.

- In the middle of the month, merge mining with Myriadcoin was discussed.

- On the 24th of June, the DigiByte Team attended the "Inside Bitcoins" conference in Hong Kong. They also visited China to gain further contacts after which time they arrived back in Hong Kong on the 30th of June.

TESTING OF THE MULTI-ALGO
HASHING ALGORITHM
JULY 2014

I.   An important status update for the community.

II.   Block reward reduced from 7,724.165174 DGB to 7,685.544349 DGB.

III.   Price of one unit of DGB account after six months of the blockchain.

IV.   Progress made with compiling the future Multi-Algo release.

V.   DigiByte Team attended the "Digital Currencies Convention for Bankers".

Some forum users on Bitcointalk were becoming worried about the lack of updates being made, especially in regards to the future Multi-Algo release. User "DigiByte" had only posted three comments within the first week on the official DigiByte thread of that forum. However, a lengthy post was submitted at the end of the first week of July (see page 78).

Blocks were still taking a long time to generate. As can be seen below, the time between the first two blocks of July was about sixteen minutes (not the specified sixty second block time):

Block # 136,513 (Reward 7,724.165174) July 1st 2014 at 12:04:59 AM UTC

Block #136,514 (Reward 7,724.165174) July 1st 2014 at 12:21:17 AM UTC

On the 7th of July at 00:30:42 UTC, user "DigiByte" said:

"Greetings Everyone,

We wanted to give everyone an update as we can see people are getting restless and the trolls are now coming out from under the bridge. We have a lot of stuff happening in the background right now & we are working very hard to get some major things rolling to take DigiByte to the next level.

We have been working on the multi-algo mining pool as well as putting finishing touches on the multi-algo update. We also have started work on the trading platform. Over the course of the last two weeks we have had several high level meetings and have been completely swamped while traveling as well as trying to do development work.

Our trip to Hong Kong for Inside Bitcoins and our journey into mainland China went very well for DigiByte. We have made friendships & partnerships to help give DigiByte a strategic global advantage over most other coins that will be leveraged in the near future.

At this point there has only been two of us that have been able to work full time on DigiByte. Others on the team have helped when they can.

Meeting with investors, merchants and others all the while trying to roll out a big update as well as maintaining a solid social media presences is a lot for two people to take on. Especially while traveling in a foreign country like China. We have since been actively going outside of the crypto world to recruit other developers, marketing professionals etc to help us out and we invite other developers and people to come on board if you believe in what we are trying to accomplish.

We have also been instructed by our main DigiPay investors to not divulge to much information until we are absolutely ready to roll. We don't want to let our competitors know exactly what we are up to right now. Plus we have signed an NDA. Things in the professional business world don't happen over night.

We agree we need to get things done as fast as possible right now and things are moving very fast in the crypto world. But we feel as long as we keep working hard toward our original goal of becoming a worldwide payment system for micro transactions we will achieve long term success.

As stated many times before we are in this for the long haul. We are now back home and getting back in the routine swing of things so our number one priority is to get the multi-algo update out and to make sure it works. We have tested it quite a few times but we wanted to organize a large scale test though a multi-algo mining pool. We want to make sure we have mining infrastructure in places when we roll out the update.

Thanks for your patience and support! Stay tuned for more updates over the next few days and lets take DigiByte to the moon!"

Block #137,759 (Reward 7,724.165174) July 7th 2014 4:15:32 AM at UTC

Block #137,760 (Reward 7,685.544349) July 7th 2014 04:54:35 AM at UTC

As can be seen yet again from the above block reduction, it was taking a very long time at this stage to generate blocks. There would not be another block reward reduction until the 2nd of September 2014.

On the 10th of July, the DigiByte blockchain had been active for six months. Bitcoin Satoshi values of one unit of DGB account on this day are shown below. MintPal and Cryptsy were the exchanges on which most trading was taking place.

	Price	Low	Open	Close	High	Volume (BTC)
MintPal	31.5	31	32	31	34	2.22407
Cryptsy	32	31	32	32	36	0.432825
Coined Up	35	35	35	35	35	0.0649909

source: www.cryptocoincharts.info

On the same day at 14:28:36 UTC, user "DigiByte" said:

"To give everyone an update:

We have set the mining pool up to organize a large scale final test.
We had planned on doing this last night but we are still experiencing an issue with 1 of the algos we are trying to work out. We hope to wrap this up today / tonight.
Then we will do a 24 hour test which we will invite everyone to participate in.
Then hopefully release the updated wallet by Saturday/ Sunday.

Then we we will have to give everyone a couple weeks to update
before the specific block of the switch kicks in."

On the 15th of July at 21:05:28 UTC, user "DigiByte" said:

> "Here is the mining information you will need to help us test multi-algo DigiByte mining. Please feel free to ask questions & help us iron out all the issues before we roll out the multi-algo update (will be called version 3.0). We will release the addresses when the pool is properly configured. We are shooting for 11 PM UTC now. Stay tuned!
>
> Mining Algorithm #1: DigiBitcoin (Sha256), Mining Algorithm #2: DigiLitecoin (Scrypt), Mining Algorithm #3: DigiGPU (Skein), Mining Algorithm #4: Digi3to1 (Groestl) and Mining Algorithm #5: DigiCPU (Qubit)."

Over the next couple of days, testing continued on the Multi-Algo hashing algorithm. Some people wanted to be paid in DigiByte as a reward for them committing costly hash towards testing. "DigiByte" referred to the pre-mine as already spent and was confident that testers would benefit in the long run from the success of DigiByte.

Problems existed with algorithms Qubit and Groestl during testing. On a particular test mining pool, there were difficulties mining DigiByte.

On the 19th of July at 20:30:20 UTC, user "DigiByte" said:

> "Great news everyone!
>
> We have finally got the multi-algo code functioning with the proper difficulty adjustments. Our previous open test revealed several issues that we have now corrected. One of the issues was making the difficulty of two of the other algos match sha's difficulty. This was obviously an issue and it was not an issue easily revealed with in house testing. We needed to have that additional hash to show how the network would really respond. So thank you all for helping with that!
>
> We are now testing some more tweaks to optimize the DigiShield performance so there is no chance of a sluggish blockchain like we are seeing now. We are also considering testing a couple other algorithms which we think will be more energy efficient for everyone's GPU's. We will make 100% sure everything works before releasing the update.
>
> Right now our goal is to finalize/release the update by Wednesday. Thank you for your patience!"

On the 23rd of July at 20:09:36 UTC, user "DigiByte" said:

> "To update everyone on multi-algo:
>
> We have the myriad 5 algo implementation working as expected but we are trying to improve that implementation even more by using other algos with better mining performance for GPU users. Will keep you all posted."

Towards the end of the month, the primary focus was to release the Multi-Algo update. They were testing the five algorithm Myriad code combination and then adding their own innovative code to create a unique algorithm specific for DigiByte.

On the 28th of July at 21:45:25 UTC, user "DigiByte" said:

> "Thank you very much for the support & kind words! We are glad to see our efforts being recognized like this. We are committed and we are working hard on several things in the background right now that will have far more impact than an algo update (although it is a big update & we should see a positive response from the crypto community at large).
>
> We just landed in New York and will be attending the first ever Digital Currencies convention for bankers tomorrow. You can find more info here:
> http://www.americanbanker.com/conferences/digitalcurrencies/
>
> This is all fitting together for DigiPay LLC as well as merchant adoption later on for DigiByte. Our goal is to have the multi-algo update released by this coming weekend.
> Thank you everyone for the support & lets keep these awesome discussions going within the community. There are a lot of very good ideas coming from some bright & talented people.
>
> Thanks you!"

Other events which occurred in the month of July:

- On the 19th of July, "DigiByte" notified people who had coins on the exchange called AGX.io to withdraw their DGB before the 31st of July 2014.

- On the 29th of July, the DigiByte Team attended the "Digital Currencies Convention for Bankers" in New York City.

PUSH TOWARDS BLOCK NUMBER 145,000
AND THE RELEASE OF MULTI-ALGO

AUGUST 2014

I.   DigiByte version 3.0.0 wallet client released.

II.   DigiByte version 3.0.1 wallet client released.

III.   DigiByte began to trade on the cryptocurrency exchange called Bittrex.

IV.   DigiByte community processing power (hash) push towards block 145,000.

V.   August ended with only 469 blocks remaining until block number 145,000.

On the first day of the month, the community were informed about the recent "Digital Currency Convention for Bankers" in New York City. User "DigiByte" was very happy to say that new contacts had been made with key players in the industry as well as the opportunity to introduce DigiByte to a wider audience. They described the event as the most beneficial and insightful event attended so far. Discussions were had, not about if digital currencies would go mainstream, but when and how they would. Other development teams from Ethereum, Mastercoin and Ripple were also present. Jared Tate was quoted as saying:

> "Some very positive things are underway.
> Finance is changing & we are proud to stand along side all of you as we are all pioneering the future of money!
>
> DigiByte to the moon!"

On the 1st of August at 22:17:24 UTC, user "canman" was quoted as saying:

> "wow Jared, nice work there. connection is the key to success and the more of it the better. great and wonderful work Jared…"

On the 6th of August at 23:15 UTC, a tweet was posted by @DigiByteCoin. It was a notification of the new upcoming update in three days time:

> "We will be releasing #DigiByte v 3.0 multi algo this Saturday! #bitcoin"
>
> https://twitter.com/DigiByteCoin/status/497159066196905984

However, four days later at 11:59:42 UTC, user "DigiByte" posted the following comment:

> "We apologize for the delay.
> We updated a couple new code changes yesterday we thought would only take a few
>
> minutes. (Bitcoin core updates) It managed to break about 10 things 😫
> We have worked through the night. As soon as we get it compiled we are going to release it. Thanks again for your paintence & support."

On the 12th of August at 08:02:41 UTC, user "DigiByte" had further encouraging news about the highly anticipated v3.0.0 update:

> "Good news! We finally have been able to compile again!
> We are still experiencing a couple random crashes, so we want to test some more in the morning. It syncs with the block-chain just fine & we are able to send/receive coins as well. Thanks again for your patience. This update has been very frustrating for us. Stay tuned!
>
> Edit: We just noticed we need to change the "Bitcoin" in the Picture as well as a few other places in the wallet."

Over the next couple of days, the development team had all five algorithms properly mining blocks on testnet. They were in the process of checking and altering the code before final testing in order to make sure it would function correctly. They were confident of its release on the 14th of August.

Another update was made in the early hours of the 14th of August by user "DigiByte". He was quoted as saying:

"We are compiling the final Windows v 3.0 release as we speak. We have ran it through several tests over the last 20 hours.
We mined on all 5 algos for 12 hours and everything worked as expected.

The hard fork will occur at block 145,000. Once the software finishes compiling we will run it through a few quick sanity checks & then we will do a soft launch on here for a few hours before announcing it on social media.

We can use all the testers and feedback we can get over the next few hours.

Thanks again everyone for your patience! We are now ready to enter the next stage in DigiBytes life!"

On the same day at 05:57:06 UTC, user "DigiByte" posted the following:

Introducing DigiByte v3.0.0 MultiAlgo

"Before we release the OSX & Linux version as well as publicly announce the release we would appreciate a few beta testers on here to run the wallet through a couple send, receive, sync & solo mining tests.
(Scrypt mining will be the only algo to mine until the others kick in at block 145,000)

As always make sure to back up your wallet.dat before upgrading!
(File -> Backup Wallet -> Select location to save to)

If you see any typo's or other mistakes in the wallet please let us know! Thanks everyone!"

...(DOWLOAD LINKS)...

Five reasons were given for switching to Multi-Algo:

1.   To update DigiShield and speed up the blockchain back to normality.

2.   The fairest PoW mining available (embraces both ASICs and GPUs).

3.   It is more secure than one single algorithm (harder for a 51% attack).

4.   Faster transaction times of thirty seconds (reduced from 60 seconds).

5.   Ability to tap into the used BTC ASIC miners market.

Unfortunately, a fork (the creation of two separate blockchains) had quickly emerged between v3.0.0 and the old version. As a result, the download links for v3.0.0 were removed. A fixed wallet client had to be compiled and uploaded.

On the 16th of August at 18:04:30 UTC, a new update was released:

Introducing DigiByte v3.0.1 MultiAlgo (16th Aug 14)

"Mandatory Update before block 145,000

Ok everyone, here are the 3.0.1 download links! If we could get a few people to help us test it before making it the official release, that would be great.
Try sending, receiving and see how it syncs. Also, try mining the other algos.
Scrypt should be the only mine-able algo until block 145,000.

We ran it through some rigorous testing the last 24 hours so we should be good to go now!
We will update the wallet language translation errors later, once we get everyone updated.

Please give us feedback if everything worked for you, especially with the OSX wallet.

It is very important we get everyone updated before block 145,000 as at that point sending coins from a v3.01 wallet to a v2.9.1 wallet or early could result in problems.

As always, backup your wallet.dat before upgrading!
(File -> Backup Wallet -> Select location to save to)"

...(DOWLOAD LINKS)...

Immediately after the release of v3.0.1, efforts began to inform exchanges and mining pools to update before block number 145,000. In return, they were politely told to notify either the community or development team as soon as they had.

On the 20th of August, the DGB/BTC trading pair was added to the Bittrex cryptocurrency exchange. Bittrex is based in Seattle, Washington. It began operations on the 13th of February in beta testing mode. Fifteen days later, twelve cryptocurrencies and twenty one trading pairs were initially made available as trading went live.

Nine days after the release of v3.0.1, five exchanges reported that they had updated. These were MintPal, Comkort, AllCrypt, Bittrex and Cryptsy, but not in this particular order.

On the 26th of August, the development team rented some extra Scrypt ASICs to speed up block generation towards block number 145,000. Over the next three days, progress had been made in terms of the network's total hash. It had reached a point at which only days remained until block number 145,000. Again, the development team thanked the cryptocurrency community for contributing the required extra hashing power.

On the last day of August at 22:18:32 UTC, user "DigiByte" said:

> "Transfer your #DigiBytes from your Android wallet to a desktop wallet before block 145k as we have not yet updated it!
>
> We just realized this may cause issues for people until we get Android updated."

There had been no block reductions during the month. However, the community were optimistic that only 469 blocks remained at the end of August until the switch to the new hashing algorithm (see below).

Also by the close of the month, the official website and Bitcointalk thread had been updated with those exchanges and mining pools which had updated.

Block #144,531 (Reward 7,685.544349) August 31st 2014 at 11:57:13 PM UTC

BLOCK NUMBER 145,000 SUCCESSFULLY REACHED

SEPTEMBER 2014

I.   Block number 145,000 was successfully reached and surpassed.

II.   DigiByte began to trade on the exchange called LiteBit.eu.

III.   DigiByte Team attended the BTC Expo in Shanghai, China.

IV.   DigiByte began to trade on the exchange called CEX.IO.

V.   A total of seven block reward reductions occurred during the month.

On the 1st of September at 15:44:28 UTC, user "DigiByte" pointed out a technical fact. He was quoted as saying:

> "T-minus 100 blocks!
>
> Fun fact: The switch actually occurs @ block 144,999 because the count starts @ "0" with the genesis block."

About three hours later, user "ycagel" enthusiastically said:

> "We are there!   145k!!   YC."

(As can be seen at the top of the next page, it was found on the 1st of September.)

Block #145,000 (Reward 7,685.544349) September 1st 2014 at 7:32:42 PM UTC

Two days later, DigiByte was added to the cryptocurrency exchange called LiteBit.eu. It is based in the Netherlands.

On the 8th of September at 16:27:17 UTC, user "DigiByte" said:

"We are working hard on making some things happen in the real world for DigiByte as we speak! The price will come with time after we have publicly announced some of the things we are working on in the back ground right now. We have a vision, we have a plan and we have been working toward the same goals since the day DigiByte was launched. We are well on our way to achieving this goal & now has never been a better time to buy

(we are buying ourselves)

We are on our way to Japan & China at the moment to meet with our partners/investors to get the ball rolling on some very exciting international developments for DigiByte.
Updates & replies to messages for the next couple days will be intermittent as it is a long way to travel.
Please note we are here and a lot of people, including people new to DigiByte are working hard in the background to make things happen.

Thank you all again for your support!"

A tweet by @DigiByteCoin was posted at 09:23 UTC on the 14th of September:

"#DigiByte will be attending @BTCexpo China this coming week in Shanghai!
Good things happening for #DGB! #bitcoin #myriadcoin #multialgo"

The development team informed the community that they would not have a booth at this event and would not be speaking. However, they would be walking around the event and giving out DigiByte stickers and promotional material. They were aware that China is the largest cryptocurrency market, so knew how beneficial attending this would be.

On the 16th of September at 09:58:58 UTC, user "DigiByte" said:

DigiByte v3.0.2 Coming Soon!

"We have decided to release a version 3.0.2 wallet after the BTC China expo. This wallet will feature two main changes and will require mining pools to update:

1) A standardized Chinese name for "DigiByte" in the DGB wallet. We will be asking several native Chinese speakers at the conference what the proper translation for "DigiByte" into Chinese characters should be. Once we decide on the correct characters we will put it into the wallet. This will dramatically help DigiByte enter the Chinese market place.

2) We will be issuing a fix for the Scrypt block issue as well as the daemon rejection issue several pools are experiencing. In the mean time we would like some feedback & help testing this fix. A big shout-out to Thrassos for pointing this out and helping us figure out this issue!

...(TECHNICAL CODE)...

The github account has been updated with this change. If we could get some mining pools to test this change & report back it would be much appreciated! Thank you all!"

On the 20th of September, the DigiByte Team were at the BTC Expo in Shanghai, China. User "DigiByte" informed the community that excellent contacts were being made to help bring the coin onto the Chinese market. This event, as well as the conference in Hong Kong a few months ago, gave the team further insight into how China views the world of cryptocurrency. At the moment, China is the predominant player in the space.

On the 22nd of September at 03:31:42 UTC, user "cryptochris88" said:

> "Any updates on China considering this:
> http://www.cryptocoinsnews.com/great-firewall-of-china-blocks-bitcointalk-org/"
>
>

In response to the above, user "DigiByte" was quoted as saying:

> "This is very interesting & brings up so very interesting questions. Overall we made several new contacts at the expo & we introduced DigiByte to many new people.
>
> The conference itself was unorganized & experienced several technical problems. It could have been managed much better. However, the quality of attendees was very good. The majority were Chinese & we gained some valuable insight in to how Chinese people not only tend to use Bitcoin, but how they view it.
>
> The Chinese tend to think of Bitcoin & Digital Currencies almost like gambling or the lottery. It will either be worth a lot or nothing. They also seem to view it as a way to move money outside of China to other countries for investments or for travel. As banking fees are pretty cheap & transactions are fast already in China there is not the motivation for fee reductions like you see in the US & Europe."

On the 29th of September at 02:27:35 UTC, an exchange called CEX.IO added DGB to their platform. Reddit user "CEX_IO" said:

> "Hey Digibyte users,
>
> Now on CEX.IO you can trade DGB/BTC and as you will already know in the Ghash.IO Multipool we already have DGB available.
>
> We are adding many new coins and fiat options to CEX.IO so we invite all DGB users to come and see.
> Mine DGB Trade DGB https://cex.io"

Throughout the month of September, there were seven block reward reductions:

INITIAL BLOCK	FINAL BLOCK	DATE OF INITIAL BLOCK	TIME OF INITIAL BLOCK (UTC)	REWARD OF EACH BLOCK	TOTAL COINS AFTER FINAL BLOCK
147,840	157,919	02/09/2014	19:55:26	7647.116627	1,372,103,816
157,920	167,999	07/09/2014	00:46:50	7608.881044	1,448,801,337
168,000	178,079	11/09/2014	18:00:14	7570.836639	1,525,115,370
178,080	188,159	16/09/2014	12:02:04	7532.982455	1,601,047,833
188,160	198,239	20/09/2014	16:14:20	7495.317543	1,676,600,634
198,240	208,319	24/09/2014	16:03:51	7457.840955	1,751,775,671
208,320	218,399	28/09/2014	16:59:18	7420.551751	1,826,574,833

DIGIBYTE BEGAN TO SEARCH FOR
MORE EXPERIENCED DEVELOPERS
OCTOBER 2014

I.   DigiByte began to search for more experienced C++ developers.

II.   Problems existed on Bittrex and MintPal.

III. Number of DigiByte mined surpassed 2,000,000,000 DGB.

IV.   A total of eight block reward reductions occurred in the month.

V.   DigiByte version 3.0.2.1 wallet client released.

New members continued to join the DigiByte community. One of the major reasons why people were showing interest was due to the fact the developers had been continuously dedicated to the coin since the beginning. On the 3rd of October at 15:23:45 UTC, user "DigiByte" welcomed user "king117" to the community:

"Welcome to the DigiByte community!

We are working very hard on several things as we speak. We currently working to bring several new members of the DigiByte team up to speak. Including some very talented & experienced programmers.

As for the price, we have given up on making predictions. We are focusing on building a very solid, reliable base to build the future of DigiByte upon! We have a very good feeling about where DigiByte is headed over the next six months!"

On the 6th of October, the team announced they were working to hire some very experienced C++ developers to help take the wallet client to the next level. As a result of the time spent searching for new talent and travelling to Shanghai in China, not much work was done on the wallet client. They emphasised that they were not short on work that had to be done, they just needed help. They politely asked anyone who has C++, iOS or Android development skills to contact them via private message as soon as possible.

Three days later, users of the exchanges Bittrex and MintPal were having problems accessing or withdrawing their DGB. Both exchanges were advised to re-download and re-index the blockchain, which should resolve the issue. In particular, there was a hard cap on the number of DGB one could withdraw in one go from MintPal.

Also on the 9th of October at 07:50:08 UTC, user "DigiByte" was quoted as saying:

"We have been working closely with native Chinese speakers and we have arrived at the name of "极特币' for DigiByte!

We also have started porting updates to v3.0.2 as well as the translation. Any feedback on the name is much appreciated!

We also have created a new build environment that will allow us to build all three OS binaries simultaneously.

v3.0.2 code:
https://github.com/digibyte/DigiByteProject/tree/3.0.2

We ask that when people encounter an error please add it to the issue que here on github:

https://github.com/digibyte/DigiByteProject/issues"

On the 11th of October, the blockchain reached a particular milestone. At block number 241,972, a total of 2,000,000,000 DGB had just been surpassed as being mined (please see the block below).

Block #241,972 (Reward 7,309.799088) October 11th 2014 at 04:54:35 PM UTC

On the 11th of October at 05:31:04 UTC, user "DigiByte" reached out to the community to expand the DigiByte team in terms of numbers and experience:

DigiByte Bug Bounties & Job Offerings
"Greeting everyone!

We are excited to announce we are now offering bug fix reward bounties! Help us fix some of the issues on Github and we will send you some DGB (50,000 DGB). We are swamped with development work on other DigiByte projects. So the more eyes we can get on the code the better!
Check out the issues here: https://github.com/digibyte/DigiByteProject/issues
Also, if you have a known DigiByte issue that is not listed there, please create a new "issue" with error & code details so we can look through it. We want to begin organizing & tracking all problems there instead of via email & pm's.

DigiByte Contract Opportunities

iOS APP: We are looking for an experienced iOS developer to develop & maintain a DigiByte iOS app. Most likely this can be done by forking the bread wallet code.
https://github.com/voisine/breadwallet

We are very willing to negotiate & pay a very fair amount in DGB, BTC or USD for this work.

Finish Android DigiByte Wallet: We are looking for an experienced Android (java) developer to help us finish the wallet & work through some of the bugs we are currently experiencing. We have a wallet partway done with our existing Android wallet. We have several errors we need to debug. We are very willing to negotiate & pay a very fair amount in DGB, BTC or USD for this work.

Full-time DigiByte Developer in Hong Kong: We are looking to hire a full time C++ developer in or around Hong Kong to work on the core DigiByte code as well as other DGB projects. This person will work out of our start-up office in HK. Pm us if you are interested or know anyone who may be interested. We will be hiring more developers in the coming weeks in Hong Kong as well!

DigiByte is finally getting of the ground & we are excited to see where things are heading! email: dev@digibyte.co for more information about these opportunities!"

In the second week of October, users were finally able to withdraw DGB (as well as see their balances) from MintPal. User "DigiByte" said the following:

> "We are glad to see people have been able to withdraw some of there coins"

On the 14th of October, Cryptsy initiated the trading pair DGB/XRP on their exchange platform (XRP is the unit symbol of Ripple).

Five days later at 06:42:58 UTC, user "DigiByte" was quoted as saying:

> "Greetings Everyone,
>
> First off, a note on the rate of DigiByte production. We have read most of the comments on here regarding the price of DigiByte and the rate of DigiByte production and we understand some of your concers. As of now we have no plans to change the rate of production as we want to leave the core protocol variables alone. We feel we are right where we need to be. We have a very powerful marketing campaigned outlined that will bring more users into DGB. Once this happens we will need all the coins we can get in circulation.
>
> Secondly, we have now pushed all the fixes for the bugs everyone has been experiencing to the master branch on github. If you are a mining pool operator please help us test v3.0.2 by building from source. If all goes well we will release v3.0.2 binaries to the public tomorrow (we have compiled and tested on all os's with no problems.) We have also updated the seed nodes to v3.0.2 as well.
>
> https://github.com/digibyte/DigiByteProject
>
> We have compiled & successfully tested the upgraded DigiByte Android wallet. We plan to put this back on the play store on Wednesday. We will be releasing the official DigiByte Wiki to the public this coming Friday. We have a lot of things going on right now in the background so stay tuned for more news!"

On the following day, version 3.0.2.1 of the wallet client was released. Users had to make sure they downloaded and installed it as soon as possible. Praise was given to "raveneye" for his contribution during its development. He had spotted one small error in the code.

On the penultimate day of October, DigiByte stood at number 98 on the website www.coinmarketcap.com in terms of market capitalisation (the total fiat value of all DGB ever mined). At one specific time on this day, the statistics on this site were:

> # 98 on www.coinmarketcap.com
> Market Capitalisation: $107,002
> Price per DGB: $0.000045
> Mined DGB: 2,364,695,165

On the 31st of October at 11:47:27 UTC, user "DigiByte" said:

> "We want to let everyone know the announcement we were planning for today has been delayed for a week do to circumstances out side of our control. Nothing bad, just timing, as well as market timing. We are working very hard on some cool projects! Stay tuned!"

Throughout the month of October, there were eight block reward reductions:

INITIAL BLOCK	FINAL BLOCK	DATE OF INITIAL BLOCK	TIME OF INITIAL BLOCK (UTC)	REWARD OF EACH BLOCK	TOTAL COINS AFTER FINAL BLOCK
218,400	228,479	02/10/2014	14:28:52	7383.448992	1,900,999,998
228,480	238,559	06/10/2014	11:27:50	7346.531747	1,975,053,038
238,560	248,639	10/10/2014	08:40:52	7309.799088	2,048,735,813
248,640	258,719	14/10/2014	06:38:01	7273.250093	2,122,050,174
258,720	268,799	18/10/2014	01:37:35	7236.883842	2,194,997,963
268,800	278,879	21/10/2014	21:43:14	7200.699423	2,267,581,013
278,880	288,959	25/10/2014	21:47:58	7164.695926	2,339,801,148
288,960	299,039	29/10/2014	17:12:05	7128.872446	2,411,660,183

By the end of the month, the official website had been re-designed and a new text logo was published (see the top of page 94). Also, the DigiByte Team asked for a moderator on www.reddit.com/r/DigiByte to help update the links and information present on there. A future DigiByte Wiki website was also in progress.

AN INVESTMENT OF $250,000 IN DIGIBYTE
AND NEW OFFICES
NOVEMBER 2014

I. Bitcoin Satoshi value of DGB doubled during the first week.

II. A new block reward scheme proposed due to hard fork at block 400,000.

III. A total of eight block reward reductions during the month.

IV. DigiByte version 3.0.3 wallet client released.

V. An investment of $250,000 and new offices in Santa Monica and Hong Kong.

The value of one unit of account of DGB had reached a low of 11 Bitcoin Satoshi by the penultimate day of October according to Bittrex. This was the lowest value since an exchange rate conversation of DigiByte against Bitcoin started.

Work had already begun on a new wallet client:

> "We will be releasing a version 3.0.3 wallet as it appears our issue with the wallet going into safe mode is not fully resolved. Some wallets are still experiencing the "Warning: Some miners appear to be experiencing problems" error.
> Thanks to raven's help we have been able to track down and isolate the issue."

At this stage, any changes to the coin specification such as block time, block reward or difficulty re-targeting were undisclosed.

Block #299,039 (Reward 7,128.872446) November 2nd 2014 at 03:15:10 UTC

Block #299,040 (Reward 7,093.228084) November 2nd 2014 at 03:18:48 UTC

The block reward continued to reduce by 0.5% every 10,080 blocks. Since the 1st of September (block number 145,000), an average block was scheduled to be successfully solved every thirty seconds (~3.5 days between block reductions).

Block #309,119 (Reward 7,093.228084) November 5th 2014 at 17:01:09 UTC

Block #309,120 (Reward 7,057.761944) November 5th 2014 at 17:01:31 UTC

Cryptsy had become the most popular exchange on which the coin was trading. In terms of BTC Satoshi, the price had risen from 12 to 24 by the 7th of November. Two days later at 16:44:56 UTC, user "HR" commented on the current price of DGB:

"Currently being bid at 24, and 4.5 million offered at 25.
Approximately another 8 million more or less evenly spread out between 26 and 29 (only referring to Cryptsy here, but Bittrex looks pretty much the same). I think someone's going to be asking themselves somewhere down the line, "why the hell did I sell at that price?"

Edit:
11 million bid at 22 on Cryptsy
10 million bid at 22 on Bittrex

22 is that old support/resistance level, remember, thus the importance of 23 trading, and now we've got SIZE bids starting at 22! That's real nice short term confirmation."

Block #319,199 (Reward 7,057.761944) November 9th 2014 at 11:40:22 UTC

Block #319,200 (Reward 7,022.473134) November 9th 2014 at 11:41:00 UTC

For the past several days, there had been problems with the official block explorer site. On the 10th of November, user "bogglor" said:

> "Doesn't work for me:
>
> 502 Bad Gateway
>
> nginx/1.6.2"

At 07:13:34 UTC on the same day, user "DigiByte" replied:

> "We have had a couple issues with the block explorer needing to be restarted every 24 hrs or so. We are working to get it functioning as expected."

In the space of twelve days, the fourth block reward reduction occurred. In order to see the next four remaining reductions of November, please see page 25.

Block #329,279 (Reward 7,022.473134) November 13th 2014 at 06:22:08 UTC

Block #329,280 (Reward 6,987.360768) November 13th 2014 at 06:22:36 UTC

On the 14th of November at 08:43:28 UTC, user "DigiByte" was quoted as saying:

> "Help us test on the DigiByte Android Wallet!
>
> We have tested several transactions to different wallets & we could use help testing a bit more before we release the wallet to the Play store. Download the APK here:
>
> http://www.digibyte.co/sites/digibyte.co/files/dgb-multialgo-test-signed_0.apk
>
> https://dl.dropboxusercontent.com/u/42300902/DigiByte_Wallets_Current/dgb-multialgo-test-signed.apk
>
> Remember to always back up your private keys before upgrading."

On the 18th of November, an independent journalist called Deemington of "CoinJoint.com" interviewed Jared Tate (interview can be found in the appendix).

http://coinjoint.info/catching-up-with-digibyte/

On the day later at 09:44:11 UTC, a proposed update at block 400,000 was made:

"Dear DigiByte Community,

DigiByte was launched on January 10th, 2014 with 60 second block times and the promise DigiByte would reach a maximum coin production of 21 billion coins about 30 years from now. There was also an understanding that roughly 4 billion coins would be produced in the first year of DigiByte's life.

As many of you are aware, following the second DigiShield update, DigiByte production came to a halt with slow block times. To return to the proper rate of production, we hard forked to MultiAlgo mining.

We successfully achieved the benefit of five mining algorithms for much faster transactions with the switch from 60 second blocks to 30 second blocks.

These faster transactions will be a huge boost in the future for merchants & DigiByte users. However, this increased coin production leaves us with a short term inflationary problem in a deflationary code environment.

With the block speed reduction (60 seconds to 30 seconds), DigiByte production doubled. This means twice as many coins are currently entering the DigiByte ecosystem as originally planned. While this originally worked to catch us up to the projected 4 billion coins in the first year, we feel with an upcoming hard fork that now is the best time to make a change. If production remains the same, we face a massive inflationary problem over the next year and we will reach maximum DigiByte production in 15 years.

We have always been opposed to intentionally increasing the rate of production, but in this case everyone wins when we reduce the current reward to fit in with our original vision and timeline. Everyone's DigiBytes will become more valuable, and our current inflation problem will be curbed by roughly two-thirds.

This will help to alleviate some sell pressure on the price.

We are proposing three major changes in this hard fork @ block 400,000:

A)Change production from 6746 DigiBytes per block at time of fork to 2435 DigiBytes per block.

B) Change reduction from 1% per week to 1% per month.

C)Update DigiByte difficulty code to prevent future time warp attacks."

On the 27th of November at 12:42:17 UTC, after tests were made on the source code, user "DigiByte" announced the anticipated new mandatory update:

> "DigiByte v3.0.3 with Hard Fork @ Block 400,000 Officially Released
>
> What is in v3.0.3?
> * Hard Fork @ Block 400,000 to update difficulty calculation
> * DigiByte reward reduction @ block 400,000
> * DigiByte Logo in Wallet
> * Old clients will be rejected by network"

One day later at 20:02:45 UTC, a mayor press release was released by the development team concerning new offices and a private investment:

> "Dear DigiByte Community,
>
> Its is with great pleasure that we make the following press announcement:
>
> The DigiByte Team is pleased to announce the opening of two new companies and offices representing their full suite of products & services:
>
> DigiPay LLC of Santa Monica, California and DigiTrade International Limited of Hong Kong. With a private investment made for USD $250,000, the DigiByte Team now has the financial backing to build software and services around the DigiByte core protocol and bring DigiByte further into the digital and real world markets.
>
> Through a strategic partnership with Tofugear Limited of Hong Kong, the DigiByte Team has now expanded to developing solutions in a global operation, to meet the ever-changing demands of the consumer. In collaboration with Tofugear Limited's strategic retail, wholesale and technical development partnerships, the DigiByte core protocol is currently being developed into a range of solutions that will revolutionize the consumer's daily life."

At the end of the month, the development team were happy with the last eleven months of progress. Many connections within the cryptocurrency world had been made as well as with real world businesses, industries and professionals. They reiterated that they would remain focused on DigiByte for the long term.

HARDFORK AT BLOCK NUMBER 400,000

DECEMBER 2014

I.   Number of DGB generated surpassed 3,000,000,000.

II.   DigiByte hardforked at block number 400,000.

III.   DigiByte began to trade on the exchange called Cryptopia.

IV.   Testing of a different type of wallet client (DigiBit) began.

V.   First Christmas for DigiByte arrived.

At the end of November, DigiByte received a private investment of $250,000 and formed a partnership with Hong Kong-based web developer Tofugear. Tofugear is based in Hong Kong. At the time, this figure was one of a few high profile funding announcements in the cryptocurrency space. In an official announcement, the developers said:

> "In collaboration with Tofugear Limited's strategic retail, wholesale and technical development partnerships, the digibyte core protocol is currently being developed into a range of solutions that will revolutionize the consumer's daily life."

This news coincided with the launch of two DigiByte-focused startups: DigiPay LLC in California and DigiTrade International Limited Hong Kong

On the 2nd of December at 12:44:56 UTC, user "24hralttrade" shared his designs of a DigiByte paper wallet. He made the following comment:

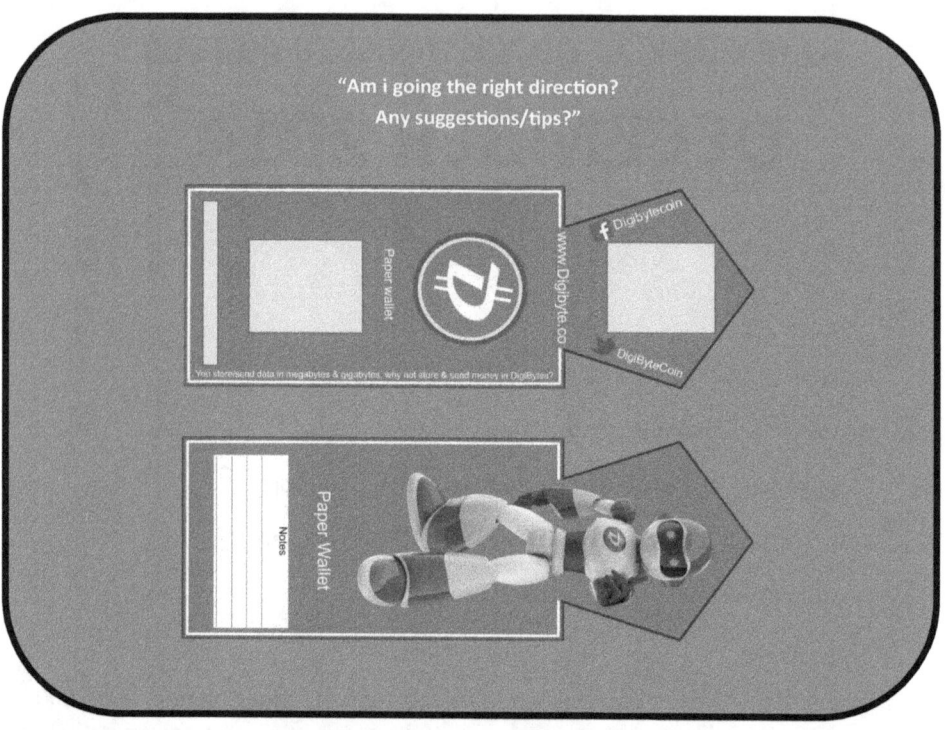

Block # 379,679 (Reward 6,848.658168) December 2nd 2014 at 18:28:29 UTC

Block #379,680 (Reward 6,814.414877) December 2nd 2014 at 18:28:53 UTC

Two days later, user "ycagel" contacted several news media sources including TechCrunch, Wall Street Journal and CBS Marketwatch. Besides these, Asian cryptocurrency exchanges called Bter, BTC38 and BTC China were also contacted. The objective was to further spread the word about the coin. Also on the 4th, the total number of DGB generated surpassed 3,000,000,000 at block number 383,532 at 05:49:58 UTC.

On the 5th of December, user "DigiByte" notified members of the community that the Android wallet had been restored:

> "Greetings Everyone,
>
> We wanted to let you know that the DigiByte Android Wallet is back on the Google Play store:
>
> https://play.google.com/store/apps/details?id=de.schildbach.wallet.digibyte&hl=en
>
> We have had a couple reports of the app crashing after the update from the old android wallet.
>
> If this is the case make sure to back up your wallet keys, uninstall that app & then reinstall from the play store.
>
> If for some reason you didn't back up your private keys PM us and we can send you an older version of the wallet to install directly in order to back up your keys.
>
> Cheers everyone!"

User "24hralttrade" kept on notifying the DigiByte community each time exchanges had updated to version 3.0.3 of the wallet client. It was on the 5th of December that all exchanges had managed to update. Cryptsy, CEX.IO, Bittrex, Comkort, LiteBit.eu were the first exchanges to do so. AllCrypt and Lazycoins were the last two exchanges to notify.

Also on the 5th, DGB were successfully sent/received from/to a prototype iPhone App. Further tests by the development team and volunteers from the community would be necessary before its future release.

Block # 389,759 (Reward 6,814.414877) December 6th 2014 at 17:58:26 UTC

Block #389,760 (Reward 6,780.342802) December 2nd 2014 at 17:58:49 UTC

By the 9th of December, user "24hralttrade" posted the following two images on Bitcointalk. One image (left) concerned the upcoming iPhone wallet and the other was designed to coincide with the current voting campaign to get DigiByte added to the international payment processing platform called OKCoin:

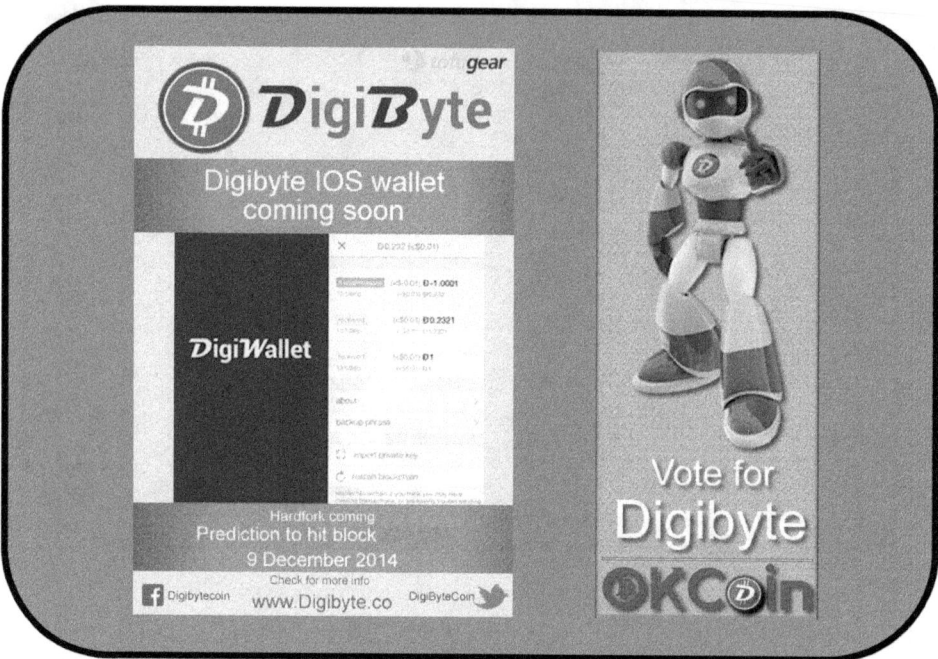

One day remained until the expected hard fork of the blockchain at block number 400,000. User "DigiByte" at 08:06:54 UTC was quoted as saying:

"Once we get through the hard fork and we make sure everything is running as expected we will be announcing some new development bounties to help get everyone more involved. These will includes, graphics, guides, translations and promo videos. So be thinking of DGB ideas

while you are mining these last few easy blocks "

Another reminder to update to version 3.0.3 of wallet client was given.

Block # 399,839 (Reward 6,780.342802) December 10th 2014 at 15:32:06 UTC

Block #399,999 (Reward 6,746.441088) December 10th 2014 at 16:51:42 UTC

Block #400,000 (Reward 2,434.41) December 10th2014 at 16:51:45 UTC

As can be calculated from the above, the block reward reduced about 64% as soon as block 400,000 was timestamped to the blockchain. Consequently, the inflation of the coin had been cut. An average block time of thirty seconds still applied. Also on the 10th of December, DGB began to trade on the exchange called Cryptopia.

On the 12th of December, testing of a different type of wallet client (DigiBit) had begun. The developers described it as:

"What is DigiBit? DigiBit is a DigiByte port of the MultiBit Bitcoin wallet. The key advantage of DigiBit is it does not require a new user to download the entire DigiByte chain. It syncs with the network by downloading the block headers only very quickly. Just as satoshi specified in the original white paper (simplified payment verification)."

On Christmas Day, user "DigiByte" at 07:21:29 UTC festively posted the following:

"Merry Christmas to everyone! The DigiByte community rocks! We are very excited to see what the new year brings!"

On the last day of 2014 at 14:59:10 UTC, user "24hralttrade" had enthusiasm as the community were looking forward to the New Year. He said:

"The future ahead, holds numerous surprises for us. Be open to changes. Wishing you all a Happy New Year. Let's break some goddamn barriers and build many bridges all the way!"

DIGIBYTE ONE YEAR ANNIVERSARY
JANUARY 2015

I.   First block of 2015 timestamped at 00:00:09 UTC on New Year's Day.

II. User "DigiByte" posted his first comment of 2015.

III. Block reward reduced by 1% for the final time during the first year.

IV. One year had passed since the blockchain began (block number one).

V.   One year had passed since the public launch of the blockchain.

On the 1st of January at 04:47:58 UTC, user "DigiByte" posted his first comment of 2015 on the official DigiByte Bitcointalk thread:

> "Happy New Year everyone! 2015 is going to be a great year for DigiByte!"

Thirteen minutes later, user "24hralttrade" said:

> "Happy new year Jared & team, thank you for last year"

The first block successfully mined and timestamped to the blockchain in 2015 was:

> Block #461,090 (Reward 2,434.41) January 1st 2015 at 12:00:09 AM UTC

Block #480,159 (Reward 2,434.41) January 7th 2015 at 03:21:54 PM UTC

Block #480,160 (Reward 2,410.0659) January 7th 2015 at 03:22:32 PM UTC

On the 7th of January, the block reward reduced by ~1% for the final time during the first year. Further reductions of 1% would occur approx. every month (every 80,160 blocks). The next reduction of 1% would occur at block number 560,320.

On the same day, user "24hralttrade" (@Alttrade) tweeted the following:

"@ShapeShift_io Would love to see @DigiByteCoin on @ShapeShift_io ,1 year of dedicated development & making big steps!"

Established in August 2014, ShapeShift is a Swiss web platform. It allows users to instantly convert one cryptocurrency into another without creating an account or depositing funds. Erik Voorhees is the founder and CEO. On the 17th of November 2015, there were a total of thirty nine different coins accepted including DigiByte.

On the 9th of January at 22:00:06 UTC, user "CryptoJohn" was the first to wish the coin a happy birthday on Bitcointalk:

"Let me be the first to wish DigiByte a happy birthday. I know I'm a few hours early but....

...(PICTURE)...

Let me be the first to wish DigiByte a happy birthday. I know I'm a few hours early but...."

Further birthday wishes were submitted on this forum as well as other social media sites. On the 10th of January at 02:13:58 UTC, user "DigiByte" said:

"Thank you everyone for the birthday wishes!
We are very proud of the fact DigiByte turns 1 year old today!
This is a huge mile stone & a testament to making DigiByte become a reality!"

Also on the 10th of January, user "DigiByte said:

> "DigiByte is officially turning 1 year old today!
> DigiByte was successfully launched on January 10th 2014 at 12 PM MST. This marks 12 months of consistent, committed development.
>
> Over the course of the past 12 months DigiByte has endured 3 separate hard forks, several updates and a very turbulent alt coin market. Through all this DigiByte is emerging as a dedicated leader in the digital currency space. We are working on several exciting projects to push DigiByte forward in 2015 and we are very excited for what the future holds!
>
> We are very committed to the long term success of DigiByte and we warmly welcome everyone into the Digibyte community!"

As soon as block number 489,636 was timestamped to the blockchain, the blockchain had been operational for one year (see below).

Block #489,636 (Reward 2,410.0659) January 10th 2015 at 10:28:25 PM UTC

Jared Tate was working on a new DigiByte video to be released soon. The DigiByteTalk forum did not really become very active since it went live back in January. Bitcointalk had been the main forum for DGB discussion. User "DigiByte" kept welcoming new members (newbies) on the official DigiByte Bitcointalk thread.

On the 12th of January, the blockchain turned one year old in terms of the time miners had been able to mine the coin. As can be seen below, the last block timestamped during the one year period of public mining (time of the blockchain excluding the developer pre-mined stage) timestamped at 17:24:44 UTC.

Block #494,764 (Reward 2,410.0659) January 12th 2015 at 05:24:44 PM UTC

A total of about 3,342,203,514 DGB had been mined as soon as block number 494,764 was timestamped. Thirty six seconds later, the next block was found:

Block #494,765 (Reward 2,410.0659) January 12th 2015 at 05:25:20 PM UTC

APPENDIX

INTERVIEW OF JARED
BY BRENDON LINDSEY
PUBLISHED ON THE
16TH OF JANUARY 2014

"DigiByte is making a name for itself, at a very rapid pace. Alongside NobleCoin, it remains the first contender of 2014. We here at Follow the Coin are huge fans of DGB, so we were glad when we were given the opportunity to speak to BitcoinTate about the new cryptocurrency."

BRENDON LINDSEY: **"You list your development team on the official DGB site. Can you give us a little info about what it is you all do?"**

BITCOINTATE: "**BitcoinTate**– Professional Web Developer who works from home & has been conducting most of the day to day DigiByte operations since launch.

The Finchster – Expert Programmer, & Independent Programming Consultant. Brilliant guy.

EDOG – Attorney at Law, hopefully keeps us out of trouble.

Giggler – Professional IT & Network Support, Alt-Coin enthusiast.

SifuGT – Sr. Project/Training Manager with over twenty years experience in a world renowned organization. He is our quality assurance guy."

"What made you decide it was time to start your own coin?"

"All the meme, joke, and scam coins were getting old. We wanted to create something with real value & potential that could be traded for goods and services. When the November price run up occurred, we decided it was time to get the project in gear. We wanted to give people a coin that was fair, had a great name, and had been well thought out."

"How happy are you with how the launch went? Did it go as you planned? Better? Worse? How did the pre-announcement affect the launch?"

"Launch was very stressful, but overall it went relatively smoothly and we are pleased. We had a slight delay getting the source uploaded to GitHub and we had one pool attacking another, but we got through it okay. Pre-announcing a coin is a double-edged sword. If you do announce ahead of time, it gives people plenty of time to rip your coin apart (which is noted in the first couple thread pages, which we refuse to delete as it is a part of history). If you do not announce a coin at least 2-3 days ahead of time, you are accused of an instamine and not being fair. More importantly, the coin is much more vulnerable to attack. We delivered at the exact minute promised, download server of course was slammed, but it held up."

"Recently, all new launches have gone through a post-honeymoon phase where, a week after launch, things quiet down with the developers, and early miners start jumping ship for the "Next Big Thing". What plans do you have to keep interest for new adapters going?"

"We plan to keep the community involved and excited about DigiByte. We have an Android wallet almost completed, thanks to some awesome community assistance. This has allowed us to bump up our launch time frame for new features like the Android wallet with a QR Code Reader. This will help more people use the coin and encourage adoption by several new merchants. We believe making DigiByte easy to use and accessible on a smart phone are huge steps toward mainstream adoption of DigiByte. We plan to use the DigiMan to teach the average consumer how to download a wallet, send & receive transactions, and much more. We want to use him to relate to the average person on the street in a simple & easy to understand manner. We have also gotten a lot of interest from merchants. Just three days after launch, you can now use DigiByte to buy web design & development services in Europe and the United States, electronic cigarettes in Australia, rent a hotel room in Portugal, buy clothing in the United Kingdom, and potentially even buy alligator meat from Florida."

"One thing I keep seeing everywhere on your site and in your forum topics is that this is a "professional" cryptocurrency. What, in your opinion, is the difference between a currency that's professional, and one that isn't?"

"First of all, the name. Do you picture your grandmother walking into a store one day and purchasing something with her BBQcoin or HoboNickels? We don't. Second of all, an unprofessional currency is one that has been launched sloppily, lacks any descriptive information of the coin, and does not have an engaged development team. Finally, the worst thing is when you download a new wallet and they didn't even bother changing the text in the wallet from the previous coin. We spent almost two weeks getting the code right in order to compile it the first time. Then we recompiled it several more times after making changes. We even re-hashed the genesis block twice to make some improvements over the first. We wanted to make a coin that would actually be used by merchants. There is huge support for alt's right now from the "real world." People are starving to support the next big thing with real world professional potential. We feel we hit the market at the right time."

"I know you planned the launch out well ahead of time. How far ahead has the development team planned in terms of new features, merchant adoption, exchanges, etc.? Is there a roadmap in place, or is it more of a reactionary plan based on what happens from here on out?"

"There is a long-term plan. We see the potential for DigiByte to be a billion dollar coin in a year or so. We have laid out our goals and steps that must be achieved to get there. Some of them include establishing a foundation, getting DigiByte tied directly to the USD, and getting as many merchants as possible to use DigiByte. We do, however, listen to the users and are flexible to changes that must occur. It definitely is not an exact science. One thing that surprised us was that people actually started complaining that we were giving away too many coins. We realized they had a valid point, and that in order to build value in the coin we needed to stop. So now bounties are given for development of the coin only. We feel we have been very generous and are down now to almost a .25% premine."

"Your site mentions the DigiByte Foundation is coming soon. What is the goal for the Foundation?"

"First, it is to legally protect the coin & developers. Second, it is to ensure a bright, long-term future for DigiByte. We are looking to the Bitcoin Foundation as an example of how to do this but this entire process is not well known as many of the governing laws are vague or have not yet been written. Setting up a foundation for a cryptocurrency is like riding through the wild, wild, west on a three legged pony."

"If users want to get involved with helping the DigiByte project or Foundation, how can they do so? Who should they get in touch with? And is there any particular set of skills you're currently hunting for?"

"Message the DigiByte account on BitcoinTalk. We have had over fifty people contribute to the coin already in a variety of ways. There are some very bright, talented community members that have started supporting DigiByte. The initial community has been fantastic and we would like to thank each and everyone one of them for their support! We are open to even more ideas and invite more people to join the team with any skill they feel they can contribute with. Our goal is to make Digibyte a coin that people can get behind and make their own."

"When we spoke with the Worldcoin founders, they mentioned that even their grandparents were buying into WDC as an investment. How many of your grandmas currently own DGB?"

"One of them received her first Bitcoins last April and is now receiving her first DigiBytes. She is a great test subject. She says she could see herself spending DigiBytes as she understands what a megabyte & a gigabyte is. She gets the logic of storing money as DigiBytes. The idea has really clicked with ordinary folks that we have pitched the idea too."

"Lastly, is there anything you want to say to users who might be on the fence about setting their miners to a DGB pool to try to sway them?"

"We are in this for the long haul. We believe Bitcoin would be perfect if three things were changed. The number of coins, speed of transactions and that Scrypt algorithm was included instead of 256. We wanted to design a currency that would ideally be traded at $1-$10 and would allow a user to walk into Starbucks and purchase some coffee with their smart phone in a few seconds. DigiByte will allow for that to happen. The ratio of Bitcoins to DigiBytes is 1 to 1000. Very easy to calculate. The average person does not really understand or like buying small ticket items with Bitcoins. Sending .001 BTC to a cashier for some groceries is a bit confusing to the average joe on the street. Spending 20 DigiBytes is much more easily understood. In the end, no one likes looking in their wallet and seeing they own only 0.001 BTC. 1,000 DGB is much more appealing. You store data in kilobytes & megabytes, why not buy goods and services with DigiBytes?"

"We'd like to thank BitcoinTate for taking the time to talk with us about DigiByte. If you're interested in DigiByte, you can learn more by visiting the <u>official DigiByte website</u>, or by keeping up with the <u>official DigiByte topic on BitcoinTalk</u>."

INTERVIEW OF JARED
BY DEEMINGTON
PUBLISHED ON THE
18TH OF NOVEMBER 2014

"Congratulations on the switch to multi-algorithm. How much work was that and were there any major complications?"

"Thank you! The multi-algo switch was very complicated. It took two of us about 3 months to figure it out, test it & finalize the release. We are still working through a few minor issues as well. Overall the most difficult part was the switch at block 145k which allowed people to begin mining DigiByte on multiple algorithms as changes had to be made throughout the entire codebase. It is much easier to launch a coin from the start with multiple algos than it is to convert an existing blockchain from one mining algo to several."

"Is Digibyte a full time project for the team?"

"DigiByte is definitely a full time project. There have been dozens of people contribute different things over the last ten months as well as two of us working full time since December of last year on the project. We are currently working to bring more experienced people into the project work full time on future developments. As we have stated since day one, we are in this for the long haul and our goal is to make DigiByte a successful world wide payment network."

"How was the Bitcoin Expo conference in Shanghai? What were you able to take away from this?"

"The Bitcoin Expo in Shanghai was somewhat disorganized but had an excellent attendee list from which we made several great connections. The biggest thing that we learned and picked up at the shanghai expo was that the Chinese view digital currencies more as a gamble or the lottery than a viable method of payment within China. They do, however, seem to think that digital currency is a good way to move money out of China to other countries. The Chinese also pronounce Bitcoin as "B 2 B." Litecoin is pronounced "L 2 B.""

"I saw you attended the Digital Currencies 2014 Convention in New York which aimed to "bring together bankers, regulatory institutions and the minds behind digital currencies". What was the general "feeling" you got from regulatory institutions and banking industry towards digital currencies?"

"We came away from the digital currency for bankers conference with a very positive future outlook for digital currencies. Existing financial institutions are very excited about the potential for block chain payment technologies to improve their KYC and AML reporting requirements. The term "live spreadsheet" was coined at this conference. It is no longer a matter of "if" banks adopt parts of this new innovative technology, but "how" and "who" will be the first to do it."

"On your ANN thread on Bitcointalk it says that Digibyte is working on its own exchange. How is progress going with that?"

"Yes, we are currently working on an exchange but we are not quite ready to open the beta version to the public. We are still alpha testing the platform, more details to come soon. We are also talking with potential banking partners and we are very much interested in talking with more banks who would like to begin entering this space."

"Any hints about what might be in store for the future?"

"We are working on several very exciting things right now but we are not ready to disclose any details at this particular moment. More details will be released in the near future. We can say one area we are focusing on besides an exchange is getting an Electrum wallet as well as IOS & Android wallets released. We want to make using DigiByte as simple & as straight forward as possible. We will also be releasing a detailed series of guides explaining how to use as well as mine DigiByte."

www.ingramcontent.com/pod-product-compliance
Lightning Source LLC
Chambersburg PA
CBHW051216170526
45166CB00005B/1926